Dark Confessions
of an Extraordinary, Ordinary Woman

Jenn Sadai

Shawna,
Your support
has been
amazing!
Love Always
Jenn Sadai

JCP
Jan-Carol
Publishing, Inc
"every story needs a book."

Dark Confessions of an Extraordinary, Ordinary Woman

Jenn Sadai

Published February 2014
Little Creek Books
Imprint of Jan-Carol Publishing, Inc

ISBN: 978-1-939289-33-9
Library of Congress Control Number: 2014931965

You may contact the publisher:
Jan-Carol Publishing, Inc
PO Box 701 Johnson City, TN 37605
E-mail: publisher@jancarolpublishing.com
jancarolpublishing.com

This book is dedicated to my Uncle Jeff, who inspired me to follow my dream of becoming a professional writer. It is also dedicated to the happiness I now have with the man who stood by my side over the course of a long, challenging journey. Most importantly, this book is dedicated to every woman who stayed in a bad relationship longer than she should have.

Foreword

Shutting the door does not close the subject. Pretending it did not happen does not hide the bruises. Denial does not make it untrue. Blaming one's self does not justify it. Believing a lie does not make it true.

Abuse.

Domestic abuse wears many faces and appears in many disguises. How does one accept the fact that being trapped means that you must set yourself free? How does one find the courage to walk away, stay away, and move away from an abusive relationship?

In *Dark Confessions of an Extraordinary, Ordinary Woman*, author Jenn Sadai presents raw and very personal experiences of living in an abusive relationship. The reader walks with her through her turbulence as she truthfully disclosures her struggles in finding the person inside of herself: deserving, worthwhile, and most of all, courageous. Her walk is a roadmap of determination and of walking away, staying away, and moving away from that abuse.

The hope is that every reader—especially those who themselves are victims of domestic abuse—will realize transformation is possible. Everyone deserves an extraordinary life—and Jenn Sadai confirms that.

Jan Howery, BS (Psychology—Marriage and Family Counseling)
Certified Hypnotist
Author, *Broken Petals*
Contributing Columnist, *Voice Magazine for Women*

Letter to the Reader

Thank you for giving me the opportunity to share my story. I hope it inspires other young women to realize their true potential and to live life to the fullest. I once thought my life was worthless, and now I believe my life story is worth sharing. I set a goal of becoming a published author when I was a little girl, but daily responsibilities sent me in another direction. I gave up on my dream until someone I love was suddenly facing a terminal illness (leukemia) at age 50. He reminded me that I was a writer and that I owed it to myself to pursue my talent. His inspiration was the boost I needed to finally go for it!

Less than two years later, my dream is becoming my reality.

This story needed to be written. I've been writing it inside my head for the last ten years. I have replayed different details of the first twenty-four years of my life over and over again in search of a greater meaning. Everything I endured built the woman that I am now, so I have no shame or regret for past errors in judgment. This book captures the good and bad of that journey in the hope of inspiring other women to find strength in adversity.

No matter what happens in your life, never give up.

Sincerely,

Jenn Sadai

Acknowledgements

Special thanks to Jan-Carol Publishing, Brian and Liz Cormier, Rahel Levesque, Jen Gardner, Deb Birchard, Paula Michaluk, and Laura Pearce for helping publish this story.

Thank you to Kim Harrison for designing the book cover and to Matthew Thomson Photography for taking my photo.

Also, thank you to all my friends and family who helped promote the book online.

Everything Happens for a Reason

Everything happens for a reason.

I wasted years of my life worrying, stressing, and second-guessing myself on every decision I made before I finally came to that conclusion. It took surviving the hardest moments of my life to learn how to simply let go and believe in myself. I mentally attacked myself for most of my teens and twenties before I learned how to love myself in my thirties.

Does this sound familiar?

Most women travel this bumpy road toward self-discovery. Too many of us allow self-doubt, foolish insecurities, and poor self-esteem into our lives somewhere between needing our first bra and buying our first vibrator. Our focus shifts toward pleasing the people around us and away from focusing on our own goals and ambitions. Most women survive these turbulent teenage years unscathed, but others become victim to their lack of self-worth.

Or maybe that was just me?

I was a dreamer when I was young. I had ridiculous goals and thought I was invincible. My parents can attest to that fact. I was fearless, adventurous, and incredibly klutzy. I climbed on everything when I was a kid, which meant I fell off everything.

I fell off the monkey bars and lost a tooth in the dirt when I was seven. I also fell off our roof when I was nine and broke my arm. I fell off the bleachers at a baseball game, I fell off our fence—which I had used as a tightrope—and I fell off a foot-high step that caused me to break my arm again. I was constantly tripping over my feet and landing on my face, but I always got up.

> *It doesn't matter how many times you get knocked down.*
> *All that matters in life is how many times you get back up.*

Over the past few years, I have discovered that most of those cheesy old clichés you hear are actually true. A *positive attitude will bring positive results*—eventually. The trick is maintaining your cheery outlook even when your world is crumbling around you, and doing so is almost as easy and as life-altering as finishing a marathon. I finished my first full marathon in 2010, but ten years before, when the building blocks of my world came crashing down around me, I lay down in the rubble and buried my face in the debris, praying that it would suffocate me.

A positive attitude did eventually earn me greater happiness than I ever thought possible, but if my life had been left completely in my hands, I wouldn't have been alive to experience the magic of the last ten years. Somehow things fell into place and I survived. I am comfortable taking credit for my recent accomplishments and consider myself to be a pretty confident woman, but there was a time where my life spiraled so far out of control that I gave up on myself. I can't even take credit for my tale of survival, because that miracle must have come from above.

I know I'm lucky to be alive.

Once I learned that my life was valuable, I started to treat it that way. All I did was change my attitude, and everything in my life magically got better. I made incredible friends, rebuilt damaged relationships, landed great jobs, and revived the overachiever that I was as a kid. Simply because I was in the right place at the right time—yes, another cliché—I am now happily married to a kind man who truly loves me.

My life is good now.

There was a dark time when I didn't think that would ever be possible. I went from being a fearless child who was ready to take the world by storm to a scared little girl who wished my life would end. I've finally regained the strength and confidence I once had as a child, which is why I am now making a career as a writer and why you are reading this novel.

In recent years, I have used my willpower and my determination to get into the best physical, emotional, and mental shape of my life. I didn't know that I even had any willpower or determination until I hit rock bottom. Those powerful qualities were lying dormant, with my confidence and self-esteem.

Ten years ago I was a drug-addicted, chain-smoking thief who willingly stayed in a physically, emotionally, and mentally abusive relationship for several years longer than I should have. Fortunately, I was lucky enough to survive all of life's tragedies despite lack of effort on my part. I allowed control over my own life to be stolen from me without ever fighting to get it back, and as a result I came eerily close to dying three times during the same year. Until I decided to share this story, no one in my life ever really knew how close I came to my final good-bye.

But I will get to all of that drama much later.

As far as I can remember, my life started off pretty good. The first nine years were spent in an average home with my two loving parents and my older brother, Michael. We went on bike rides together, we shared fantastic family vacations, and we actively participated in each other's lives. We even ate dinner together at the kitchen table. I didn't understand the value of a close-knit family until I went without it. Life during those first nine years seemed perfect from what I can recall.

My parents however were not perfect.

Unfortunately—like every other person alive—they were born with numerous flaws that their idolizing children found hard to accept. My mom was exceptionally young when she learned she was about to make the life-long commitment of raising another human being, and this event affected her decision-making ability during most of my upbringing. She was smart, but she was a teenager trying to be a wife and a mother. It was too much to expect from any young girl, even one as wonderful as my mom.

She was only fifteen when she found out she was pregnant.

I remain convinced that there is no fifteen-year-old in this world who is capable of making such a huge sacrifice without making some major mistakes along the way. You are still a child at fifteen. Michael was not born until after she turned sixteen, but his birth still meant that her wild yet necessary teenage years were drastically cut short.

My very Catholic, good-girl mother was knocked up by a rebel without a clue, and the only answer her family offered was immediate marriage. This was back in the late seventies, and an unwed mother was unacceptable in the eyes of her family and the rest of society.

My mom also didn't have the freedom to choose whether or not she wanted to become a mother. Less than a month after she celebrated her sixteen birthday, my mother pledged eternal devotion and commitment to my father. She then gave birth to my older brother just a few short months later. It should not come as a shock to anyone that this union tragically ended in violent threats, alcoholism, and a destructive love affair.

My parents can be best described as Sandy and Danny from the hit musical *Grease*. My mother was a sweet girl who skipped a grade and had a bright future ahead of her. My father was a troublemaker who failed a grade and was struggling to finish high school. They were complete opposites.

Surprisingly the sudden marriage brought out the good guy in my father and the wild child in my mother. He tried to be a father and a husband despite his lack of education and social skills. My mother wanted more from her life and knew she no longer wanted to be with him. Simply put, the relationship wasn't working, and my mom wanted out.

They tried a trial separation at first, but my mom wasn't willing to settle for less than she deserved in life. I am a firm believer that happiness supersedes the bonds of matrimony, and I understand her decision. Like most women in her mid-twenties, she wanted to explore her options in life. She could do that only if she divorced my father.

My father was not interested in exploring his options.
He wanted to be with my mom and only my mom.

My father loved my mother deeply and enthusiastically embraced his role as head of the house. He didn't take the news that she was leaving very well. Although I didn't know what was happening at the time, I do remember my father yelling at my mom and then punching a hole in their bedroom wall. He also used a baseball bat to destroy a slatted wooden awning we had in our backyard. My brother and I weren't really kept in the loop at first, but we could tell he wasn't happy with her decision.

The next thing I remember was her leaving.

My father *was* a good provider (unfortunately *was* is the appropriate tense because he is no longer that way), and I remain convinced that he still wishes he was with her. Sadly she had fallen out of love with him, and nothing would change it.

That is if she ever loved him in the first place. She was an incredibly young teenager when they married, and most teenagers have distorted ideals about being in love. I know I didn't understand real love until my late twenties, and I think it is safe to assume my parents didn't either.

They felt forced together by her pregnancy, and you can't force two people to stay together for very long if either wants to break free. My mom wanted to be free.

My mother's decision to leave him shattered my dad's world. It sent him into a vengeful, alcoholic binge that turned my perfect childhood upside down. My father was furious and punished my mother by insisting on custody and restricting her visits with us. He threatened to take us away from her permanently if she didn't play by his rules.

My mother has always lacked a strong backbone, and she allowed my dad to take control of raising us. In her defense, it would have been fine if he had continued to be the father I knew at that time. Unfortunately he started drinking heavily, and he was not home nearly as often as he should have been.

He was angry and drowning his sorrows.

I get it now, but I didn't when I was nine years old. My dad's heart had been ripped from his chest, and he felt that everything he ever worked for was stolen from him by the woman he loved most. I don't blame him for his mistakes at that time in his life, and I have forgiven him for his past bad judgment. I too have fallen victim to a shattered world, so it is hard for me to still hold him responsible for the past.

Unfortunately, my brother and I took advantage of our new-found freedom in all of the wrong ways. Prior to my mom leaving, we grew up with our mother being the stronger influence in our lives, and we were academically and morally beyond our years. I can now willingly confess that I was one of the biggest nerds in my grade school.

There is no shame in being smart.

In fourth grade, I even volunteered to stay in at recess to work on an extra-credit assignment. A poem I wrote about the joy of homework was hung in the classroom for all my peers to see. It is pretty surprising that the first time I was beat up wasn't until much later on in my life for completely different reason, long after I had broken free from my geeky reputation.

Michael's and my rebellion started off mildly enough, but it increased dramatically in only a couple of years. By the time I was eleven, I was sneaking booze from my father's ample supply any chance that I got—which was despicably frequent—and I made new friends with other troubled preteens in my neighborhood. I quickly became popular because I had the 'fun' house; the one without any parental supervision.

It was every young person's dream!

I particularly remember one party that quickly spun out of control to the point of absurdity. At age eleven, I didn't have much common sense, and I allowed my friends to do whatever they wanted with little concern for my family's property. A drink was spilled on our sofa without being cleaned up, someone poured alcohol into my dad's fish tank, and someone else used a bottle of whiskey to water my dad's plants.

Almost anything sounds like a good idea when you are young and unsupervised. We thought that cracking eggs into shot glasses and then dumping them on one another was a great way to waste away a hot summer's afternoon. In reality, it was a great way to waste a carton of my father's eggs.

This is how ridiculous our rebellion had become because we were too immature and young to have any clue how to handle being drunk. We behaved like the misguided boys in *The Lord of the Flies* would have if they had discovered alcohol.

I could not hide my misbehavior for very long.

Eventually the local police were knocking at my door because my new best friend had been hospitalized due to alcohol poisoning. She was drinking heavily at my house and suddenly started to convulse. Her body was shaking fiercely and mine quickly followed suit. We picked up her weak, limp shell and threw her—fully clothed—into my shower.

Unfortunately it didn't work. She was still unresponsive, and panic was setting in among my eleven- and twelve-year-old party guests, who were watching this tragedy unfold. Unwilling to call for medical help (in fear we would be punished for drinking underage), we carried my friend to her parent's house about a block away and placed her on their porch.

We rang the doorbell and quickly took off running.

It was not one of my finer moments in life. My excuse is that I was a drunk twelve-year-old, which I still feel is a strong argument, despite the fact that I no longer believe in making excuses for my behavior. I am fortunate and grateful that her parents made it to the hospital in time.

Our stupidity could have ended tragically.

This should have been a turning point in my own life that put me back on the right track. An event like that should cause you to smarten up and make better decisions before something horrific happens. Unfortunately, I was only twelve years old. For the same reason my parents struggled in their roles as husband and wife, I struggled to see the lesson in the situation.

We were too young for the task at hand.

Instead of nipping my bad behavior before it got really out of hand, this experience fueled the fire of my rebellion from my parents. My father had to talk to the police when he returned home from his own binge drinking, and he was less than thrilled that I put him in that predicament.

We both felt like we had been let down by the other, and we lashed out in a fit of anger. Words were said that I have since blocked from my memory. Or maybe I simply don't want to reveal what was said, so that our shame is not immortalized in print. Either way, they were words that should never be shared between father and daughter.

At first I took off running and hid at a friend's house, but eventually I had to go home. My brother called my mother while I was hiding out and advised her of the 'incident.' My family then decided—without consulting me—that I should live with my mom instead.

My brother was right. I was clearly not being supervised by my father, and I obviously lacked the maturity to appropriately care for my own well-being. A year and a half before I finished grade school, I switched schools and moved into a townhouse with my mother.

The new neighborhood—which was less affluent than the middle-class suburb I shared with my brother and father—gave me a chance to reinvent myself. I was the new kid, and I had the power to erase my past. I could create the image that I wanted. I knew I didn't want to go back to being a nerd that people picked on, so I opted to brand myself as a 'bad girl.'

I drank, I smoked, I stole, I got into fights, and I hung out with kids who were on similar dead-end paths. I still maintained good grades in school, but my extracurricular activities should have been a real cause for concern—if anyone had been paying attention.

My mom worked a full-time job, plus had the typical social life of a recently divorced woman in her late twenties. She talked on the phone with her friends, shopped, cleaned, and read books in her room. She also had a creepy boyfriend who took up a good chunk of her time. I didn't show any interest in doing things with her, so she kept to herself.

I tried not to give her any reasons to be concerned.

I was able to still pass as a 'good girl' in front of those who mattered. I attended church, brought home impressive report cards, and helped her around the house. I was even our class valedictorian in eighth grade, although I must admit that I didn't technically earn it. It was determined by a class election, and I used a sob story to sway votes. As one of the few kids—at that time—who came from a broken home, it was easy to play the victim and gain sympathy. I learned early on that I could get away with more if people felt sorry for me.

By the time I was in ninth grade, I had started smoking pot and had several encounters with our local police officers. Most were for minor things like egging a mean old man's house and passing out a former friend's phone number to random guys at the mall, but my mom should have taken them more seriously than she did. I was headed toward disaster, and no one seemed to notice. I still don't know if I was simply clever enough to fool the adults in my life or if no one was really paying attention to what I was doing.

Somehow I doubt that I was really that clever as a preteen.

My downward spiral escalated as I started noticing the flaws within my mother. I love my mom and I always will, but she was not the strong role model that I needed during my crucial teenage years. In her defense, she was trying to be a mother during her crucial teenage years, so I guess I had it easy in comparison.

My mom's boyfriend was still married—to my friend's mother; he was physically destructive and (I suspect) abusive as well. He once stole my mother's jewelry box (in fear that she still had her wedding ring), and he lost my baptismal jewelry in the process. He cut out all the images of men from the family pictures in her photo albums. He repeatedly called her even after she hung up the phone on him, and he once broke down our door in the middle of the night.

She acted like this type of behavior was acceptable by staying with him.

I remember one particular day that should have been a red flag that she was in an abusive relationship. I was having my first sleepover with several new friends from my school. We were watching scary movies and gossiping about the boys we liked and the girls we didn't.

It was a typical and relatively innocent eighth-grade get-together.

Then my mom's boyfriend started calling the house. We could hear her yell at him loudly, and then she would hang up the phone on him. The phone would ring again almost immediately; she'd yell something else at him, and then hang up again. After about half a dozen phone calls, he showed up at the door. He pounded on it loudly as he screamed for my mom.

He finally went away, but I was already humiliated in front of my new friends.

As an adult who has survived abuse, I now realize how poorly she was being treated. I hope my mom now realizes it and has found the true happiness she deserves. I still worry that her confidence is fragile. Hopefully I am wrong, because she is a remarkable woman who should be proud of herself. She's survived many tragedies and keeps pushing forward.

I also know how easy it is to allow someone to abuse you. I don't judge my mother for her past mistakes or for allowing so many undeserving men to take advantage of her insecurities. It is amazing what women will put up with when we think we are in love.

However, hers was definitely not the example that I needed to see at that impressionable time in my life. Watching my mother's relationship led me into my first abusive relationship when I was only fourteen years old. It should have been a meaningless childhood crush, but my taste in boys was warped. The first boy I kissed was very troubled, and that pattern continued until I met my husband ten years later.

My mother was gone out as usual, so I invited my new boyfriend over to hang out. We were sitting on the couch watching TV when we started to kiss. I was too shy and insecure in my body to allow him anything more than a kiss, but his hormones obviously wanted more. He became aroused while we were kissing, and he started to creep up my shirt. I was uncomfortable with the direction he was taking, so I pushed him away. He did not respond very well to my rejection.

He became irate and started demanding more from me.

"Why would you invite me over when your mom was not home if we were not going to do it?"

I still remember his exact words, because I couldn't believe that he actually assumed I was willing to have sex with him after only weeks of dating when I was so incredibly young. The thought had never crossed my mind. Since my mother had gotten pregnant at fifteen, I knew having sex was not something that I was willing to do until I was much older and in a real, trustworthy relationship. I was a foolish teenager, but I still had some common sense and self-respect.

Unfortunately, my boyfriend at the time did not appreciate my logic.

He chased me around the house, and I ended up locking myself in my bathroom, screaming for him to leave. I was terrified because I had no idea what he was capable of doing, since I hardly knew him. He finally gave up and left, but sadly that is not the end of the story.

When I decided to end the relationship the following day, he responded by using a metal rod to beat my face repeatedly while a crowd of teenagers watched. Fortunately, two very nice girls from my new school saw it happen and brought me home. I was quite dizzy from absorbing multiple shots to my face. My mother opened the door to see me standing there with a swollen lip, a black-eye, and a blood-soaked t-shirt. I still remember that the shirt was white and that it was one of my favorites because it made my breasts look big.

I was upset that my ex-boyfriend had ruined my shirt.

At that moment in my life, I swore it would be the last time anyone threatened or physically attacked me. I even started lifting weights in our basement, and for the first and only time in my life, I developed six-pack abs and had a pretty solid punch. I would never let anyone beat me again.

I was physically stronger, but emotionally I was falling apart.

My high-school years were filled with conflicting emotions, since I lived two very distinct lives. I excelled in school, and I was involved in various committees and clubs like music and drama. I had some good, honest friends that I could rely on, and I have kept in touch with them to this very day. Unfortunately, when I came home at night, I hung out with a less-respectable crowd, and my 'dirty deeds' became quite shameful and deceptive.

I had a part-time job answering phones at a pizza place, but it only paid around forty dollars a week. My alcohol, cigarette, and marijuana habits cost significantly more, so I needed a way to subsidize my income. I started stealing from a nearby mall and then selling the items to my friends for half the price the store was charging. I would also sell joints to friends to cover the cost of my own drugs. Balancing the 'good girl' routine in front of my boss, teachers, and family while maintaining my street credibility took skill and planning.

Somehow I pulled it off—for a little while.

One day after slipping a few lip glosses into a pocket at Shopper's Drug Mart and then moving on to the Dollar Store to pocket a few lighters, a security guard from the Shopper's Drug Mart that I was previously in grabbed my arm. He saw me take the lip glosses and followed me into the next store.

I had spent the last hour filling each pocket with a variety of goodies that I would later swap for much-needed cash. When the overweight and exceptionally agitated man searched my purse and pockets, there was over $100 in 'free' merchandise. He also found a half empty pack of cigarettes that would have contained a marijuana joint if I had not sold it an hour earlier.

I was brought into this tiny back-room office where he lectured me and told me I was forbidden from ever returning to that particular Shopper's Drug Mart. He threatened official charges but decided that releasing me to my parents was punishment enough.

He didn't know that neither of my parents ever followed through on their punishments. To make sure I did what I was supposed to do, one of them would have needed to stay home long enough to watch me. Their own social lives and responsibilities superseded teaching me a lesson, and I had my freedom back within a few days.

I may have been a fast learner in school, but it always took a few attempts before life lessons sunk in.

Three days after the mall incident, I stole a pack of cigarettes from a counter display in a hotel lobby. I was a darts player as a kid (proud English heritage), and I was out of town with my league for the Ontario championships. Neither of my parents went on the trip. My friend Sue's mother was the chaperon for several of us, and once again, I had no real supervision.

I always tested the limits when I knew no one was looking.

After the first day of the tournament, I went wandering around the hotel with Sue, and we ran into the older guys in our league. They were drinking in a lower-level hallway. I immediately joined the party and helped myself to some of their booze. Apparently I helped myself to a little too much, since I got sick later that evening.

I threw up in my suitcase, which was full of the clothes I needed for the weekend. I also smashed my head on the back of the hotel toilet and cracked the lid into two pieces. I even lied to my chaperone and blamed our coach when she asked me who gave me the alcohol.

I was a mess.

It is no shock that I was kicked out of the league after that shameful weekend. I was so embarrassed when my grandparents found out. It was my grandpa's legion, and we had played darts together there since I was a little girl. This ugly incident was followed by an even more embarrassing episode the following week in Windsor with some of my less-than-wholesome friends. We were doing shots of Blue Curaçao and tequila at a friend of my friend Katie's house.

After doing several rounds of this nasty combination, I got dizzy, so my wise friends tossed me onto a waterbed. My stomach disapproved of their decision, and everything that I had just drunk ended up all over me and the bed. The waterbed's owner was Shannon, and she was a loud and violent troublemaker who did not appreciate the blue spew in her bed.

I was kicked out of her house immediately.

Katie drove me home, but I couldn't actually go inside my house. I was disgustingly drunk, and I had chunks of blue vomit in my hair. My mom was home, and I couldn't risk her waking up, especially since I was supposed to be sleeping at Katie's house.

In my drunken brilliance, I made the decision to sleep in our shed and use the lawnmower as a pillow. I was covered in spider bites when I woke up, and I had to wear long-sleeve turtlenecks in August to cover up the welts on my skin.

Once again, this was not one of my finer moments in life.

Luckily, my own common sense finally kicked in. I was starting to realize the negative consequences of my behavior. Shannon, the same girl who kicked me out of her house for puking, later jumped me from behind at a public festival and split my right nostril open. On a different occasion, I watched her kick a guy's head repeatedly into a curb, after which he was hospitalized for a few weeks. I was surrounded by the wrong people and putting myself in danger.

I was no longer feeling comfortable with the choices I was making.

Just before I turned seventeen, I made a commitment to myself that I was going to change the path I was on. I was smart, talented, and creative. I had the potential for a bright and successful future as a writer. I also knew that if I didn't soon change the way I was living, I would ruin my life permanently.

I wasn't even seventeen years old, and I had already been involved in two incidents involving guns. Once I was walking with someone when he pulled a gun on someone else—as a threat; thankfully there was no intention of firing it. On the other occasion, a guy from my grade school once opened his door with his gun drawn because he was high and extremely paranoid.

I hate guns and didn't know either guy owned one until it was drawn. Although the gun was never meant for me, I was too close to people who owned them. I knew I would end up dead or in jail if I kept following the same path. It was time to smarten up and start hanging out with less-dangerous people.

Within a few weeks of making this crucial decision to save my life, I met the man who would almost destroy me six years later.

I went with a bunch of my 'good' friends from high school to our local laser-tag arena. We never actually played laser tag—instead we hung out in the arcade area and played air hockey, hoping to meet new guys. It was a few weeks before my seventeenth birthday, and our city didn't have many legal opportunities for teenagers to have a good time on a Friday night, so that was our form of entertainment.

That was the night I met Shane Brian Rivard.

2

Shane Brian Rivard

Shane was very attractive. He had light brown hair and piercing blue eyes. He was somewhat short (maybe an inch taller than me) but physically strong. He had an inviting smile and a seductive charm. We chatted on and off all night, exchanged phone numbers, and made plans to get together a few days later. He preferred my friend at first, but I was able to win him over pretty quickly.

Our first real date was a double date with my friend Katie and Shane's friend Jason. Katie and Jason didn't know each other prior, and they didn't really hit off. On the other hand, Shane and I both felt an instant attraction. We went for coffee and then drove around the city for a few hours. Conversation came naturally, and we shared many of the same ideals.

He admired my new plan to clean up my act, and it inspired him to do the same. Every illegal activity I did in my youth, Shane had taken it to the next level. While I was stealing $10 t-shirts from Suzy Shear, Shane was busting in a convenience store window and stealing everything he could get his hands on. His home life was considerably more dysfunctional then my own and, as a result, he had slipped further into a life of lies, drugs, and crime.

I am not making excuses for the past behavior of either of us, but children need appropriate supervision and rules. My greatest pet peeve is parents who let their children do whatever they want, whenever they want.

Children need discipline and structure.

I still do not feel like I am qualified to be a parent, and that is one of the many reasons why I do not have my own children. I have a full-time job just being responsible for me. I am too focused on achieving my own goals to be a good mom.

Shane might have been a troublemaker, but he was sweet as pie to me. He was eighteen years old and knew how to be romantic. We would talk on the phone for hours, go for coffee, and go for long drives together. He sent me roses for no reason and would hold my hand or stroke my hair while we watched TV. He even packed surprise picnic lunches for us.

I had the best boyfriend ever.

On the eve of my seventeenth birthday, he knocked on my window in the middle of the night with a basket full of food. He had sneaked off with his mom's car because he said he couldn't stop thinking about me. He took me to the beach for a midnight picnic under the stars. That was when he officially asked me out. Most guys that age would never dream of doing something that romantic, so I felt very lucky.

He also wrote me love letters, and he sang to me while he played his guitar. Shane was a talented musician, and I quickly fell head over heels in love with him. We were both trying to be better people, and—together—we started to straighten out our lives.

At the time, I was convinced that Shane had the utmost respect for me. However, it has been so long now since I believed there was any truth behind his actions that now I wonder if I was naïve right from the beginning. Whether true or not, I believed— at that time—that Shane was willing to do the one thing that so many other boys his age would not do.

Shane was willing to wait to have sex.

I don't mean wait a few dates or a few weeks. I made Shane wait a whole year. He made it an entire year of rubbing up against each other without any release. I was still a virgin and not willing to let that go so easily. Plus my fear of pregnancy was always stronger than my desire to keep a relationship.

Don't get me wrong—back then, I did want kids one day. I had this idealistic vision of growing up to be a successful writer and an incredibly involved mother. When I was in ninth grade, I mail-ordered a series of children's books and started a hope chest for my future kids. I had baby clothes, blankets, books, and toys all tucked away for when I was ready. Ten years later, I gave it all away to a pregnant friend after I had my second miscarriage.

I'm getting ahead of myself again.

I let my guard down with Shane, because I was convinced he sincerely wanted more from me than just sex. I believed he cared about me deeply and that we had a special connection. All my previous boyfriends had dumped me because I couldn't be sweet-talked into sex. Well, except for a guy in ninth grade—he dumped me because I made him feel so good about himself that he finally had the guts to ask out the girl that he really liked. In short, my track record sucked, and Shane seemed to be a genuinely great guy.

Great guys can still have flaws.

Shane was struggling to change his life more than I was, since his home life was only getting worse. We both completely stopped smoking marijuana, although neither of us tried to quit smoking cigarettes. We limited our drinking and partying to only on the weekend—a significant reduction—and, on top of that, I was the designated driver quite often and would only have a couple drinks (if any) anyway.

I stopped stealing, and I didn't steal again until the weekend—seven years later—that I hit rock bottom. I haven't stolen anything since that incident. I've always been too ashamed to admit to current friends that I was a thief, since this behavior shows such a lack of character and respect for others—but there is no point in having secrets in a book that has the word "confessions" in the title. As an adult, I've been accused of stealing two different times when I didn't, and even though I was innocent on both occasions, I felt like I had no right to defend myself because I once was a thief.

I thought Shane had quit stealing, since that was something he had promised when we made the pact to redirect our lives onto a better path. However, much later on in our relationship, he confessed that he still stole from people. When he was young, he stole from neighbors and his mom. When we lived together, he stole from me.

Obviously, I didn't know about his stealing when it was happening.

And I didn't really do anything to stop it once I realized what was going on.

In the beginning, I believed Shane was changing. He said all the right things, and I trusted him. Maybe Shane was trying and struggling. Maybe his efforts were sincere at the time, and maybe his repeated devastating misfortunes brought out the evil inside of him. Maybe he had always been losing his mind and I didn't see it. I'll never know for sure, but a part of me believes it is easier to think that the first few years were real, so that at least I feel sympathy for his faltering rather than rage for his deception.

There was deception throughout our relationship, but I didn't clue into most of it until much later on.

Shane's intentions always seemed good, and not everything that went wrong was necessarily his fault. I remember the first concert we attended together. It was August 22, 1998, and the weather was horribly humid. I was working crazy hours at the time, and it was a last-minute four-and-a-half-hour trip to a small city just past Toronto. Pearl Jam was playing with a bunch of bands, including Cheap Trick. It sounded like so much fun when Shane first told me about it. He told me that I deserved to treat myself because of how hard I've been working.

He was literally jumping up and down in excitement when his friend offered him the tickets. Seeing him that excited made me excited. The tickets ended up costing almost double the price Shane originally told me, but I didn't care. For once in my life, I wasn't really worried about the money. I love Pearl Jam, and I really wanted to watch them perform live. I honestly deserved to treat myself, so I did.

Of course, I treated Shane as well.

I worked nine hours on Friday and got home just after 6:00 pm. The plan was to drive to Toronto, find a hotel, and then go to the all-day concert on Saturday. We planned to drive home after the concert, so I could get some sleep before I had to work at the golf course at 3:00 pm on Sunday. Shane had good intentions, but he never really thought things through. I guess I am guilty as well, since neither of us really calculated the likelihood of our plan working out.

I suggested booking the hotel in advance, but Shane insisted that there were countless hotels in Toronto and that it wouldn't be an issue finding one. That was our first bit of misfortune. Apparently, no hotels in Toronto have open space on a Friday night. Hotel concierges will even laugh at you when you ask if they know of any hotels in the area that might have an open room. We tried six hotels before deciding to drive directly to Barrie.

Barrie also didn't have any available rooms, and it was now after 3:00 am.

We decided to sleep in the car—a tiny Ford Escort—which was exceptionally uncomfortable, especially after driving around for almost eight hours. I hardly slept despite being completely exhausted from work. Shane did his best to make me comfortable, and he actually managed to sleep most of the night.

He repeatedly apologized for not booking a hotel.

After the rough night of attempting to sleep, we had to spend almost three hours in an outdoor line that was not moving. We were both starting to smell really bad from sleeping in our sweaty clothes. Sadly, we weren't the only ones who were sporting a foul odor. Thankfully, Shane did his best to keep me entertained in line, and it wasn't so bad.

When we got inside the concert, he made his first real misstep. I could not find the energy to join the crowds by the stage when we first got inside, so we sat by a tree on the outskirts. My sweet boyfriend allowed me to fall asleep on his thigh, which—surprisingly—I was able to do.

Shane's leg was no longer under me when I woke up from my outdoor snooze.

He had gone off to get a beer. After panicking for about ten minutes, I saw him saunter over from the concession stand. I ripped into him the moment that he got close enough for me to do it quietly. Apparently Shane didn't know that you should never leave a woman alone in a public place when she is sleeping.

I forgave him by the time Pearl Jam started, and we enjoyed most of the concert together. There was some overly aggressive pushing and shoving, but Shane kept me protected. There were so many moments in the beginning of our relationship like the concert that showed Shane truly cared about me.

Unfortunately, his good intentions were often met with poor judgment. Shane and I were both too tired to drive home safely after the concert. We were just over four hours from home and it was already after midnight. We ended up deciding to sleep in the car again for a few hours.

We finally headed home at 7:00 am on Sunday.

We were both tired, but Shane was in a great mood because of the concert. He was a musician, and he loved every minute of the experience. I loved some moments, but my mood wasn't as cheery.

I was frustrated because I knew that I had only eight hours before I needed to be at work. I also knew that I would be working from 3:00 pm until 9:00 pm or later that night and then I needed to be back at the ad agency by 8:00 am Monday morning. I had just finished high school, and I was working 50-plus hours a week to save up for college.

I needed to get some real sleep.

I remember suggesting that we stop for gas at the first rest-stop we passed, but Shane assured me that he had plenty. He didn't want to stop because he was anxious to get me home. He knew I needed sleep. I was exhausted and attempted to rest in the car, which meant I stopped paying attention to what he was doing until I noticed that the gas light came on.

He assured me he could make it to the next rest-stop.
Unfortunately, Shane was wrong.

We ran out of gas about 25 miles from the next rest-stop. I was furious and not afraid to hide my frustration. We had to hitch a ride with a transport truck to the rest-stop, run across the busy highway, fill up a container with gas, hitch a ride back to our car, and then run across the highway for a second time.

Fortunately, we survived the experience, and the only casualty was a hole in my pants. I ripped them in the crotch when I jumped out of the massive transport truck. I got home at 2:50 pm and ended up being twenty minutes late for work. I was ridiculously exhausted while I was waitressing and even worse the next day. But Shane's intention was good, and it was hard to get mad at him for it.

Shane had tried to make me happy the entire weekend.

I wish I could say the same about the rest of our relationship. The beginning of our relationship would have made a good romance novel. In fact, we were together for almost two years before his violent temper was directed at me. Early in our relationship, I saw Shane's temper directed at his mother, but she gave him legitimate reasons to lose his cool.

I respect my mom too much now to go into the details of our problems from the past, but when I met Shane, I was not particularly fond of my own mother and her poor decisions. However, even then I felt blessed to have her instead of Shane's mom as a role model. My mom would have won Mother of the Year if she were up against Shane's mom.

Shane's mother had her own baggage from failed relationships, and she took it out on Shane. When he decided to go to college, she threw his books in the trash. When she got mad at him one night for no reason, she threw a coffee pot at his head in front of a roomful of his friends. We caught her putting estrogen and prescription painkillers in Shane's food. She constantly called both of us horrible names, and she once shoved me when I was standing at the top of their stairs. Fortunately, I caught my balance and wasn't physically hurt by her little tantrum. She was a violent, delusional woman, and living with her was making it hard for Shane to find hope in his own life.

Shane's mother wasn't his only parental issue.

The first time I met his father was almost two years into our relationship, when Shane's dad drove into the middle of their front lawn and locked the keys in the car—with the engine running. It was an old minivan, and I was the only one small enough to crawl through the back window to get the keys out. Shane's father was a drunken mess who was not sober often enough then to play a significant role in Shane's life.

It is not surprising that Shane had emotional baggage of his own.

It was somewhere around our two-year anniversary when Shane's slip-ups began to outweigh his efforts to become a better man. Up until that point, he had been flawed but loveable. I empathized with his life experiences. I thought if I showed him that I believed in him, he would soon believe in himself as well. My life was back on track, and I thought I could do the same for him.

Too many things beyond our control got in the way of him seeing the good in life.

The first time Shane's temper was directed at me was on our first real vacation together. Shane was having a hard time keeping a job—a reoccurring problem—and I agreed to treat us to a romantic bed and breakfast getaway. The place was this breathtaking cottage home on the water, and the experience was beyond our expectations—until the second-to-last day.

We went away with my closest friend, Samantha, and her boyfriend, Dave. I paid for our share of the gas, I paid for our meals, I paid for our alcohol, and I paid for our room.

Shane wanted to rent a jet ski.

I had already spent a significant amount of money on the vacation, and I have always struggled financially, so I explained that I couldn't afford to spend any more money on our summer getaway. Shane did not like that answer. He felt I was being unfair and slammed his beer hard enough for it to bust the bottle. A huge fight followed during which he squeezed my arm so aggressively that it left a bruise. We broke up a few days later.

I still had a backbone at that point in our relationship.

Unfortunately, it wasn't strong enough. I should have held my ground, but his apology and promises to try harder were believable enough— eventually—that they inspired my forgiveness. After a few weeks of enjoying the single life for the first time in two years, I went back to Shane.

The next few months went pretty smooth except for a blow-up when I had my first miscarriage. I had a positive pregnancy test, told Shane about it, and then six days later I was bleeding like a normal period.

The doctor couldn't say for sure what happened, because the pregnancy test he took was negative. Shane wasn't sure if I was lying about the positive test, if I aborted the child without him knowing, or if I did something intentionally to miscarry. None of these things were true, but it was hard to convince Shane of anything once he was angry.

For some strange reason, Shane was actually thrilled that I was pregnant.

I felt we were way too young, and I was petrified by the idea, but he was calm and ready to take on the responsibility. When I told him that I was no longer pregnant, he accused me of doing something to cause the miscarriage because he knew that I didn't want to be pregnant in the first place.

Shane went out drinking for a couple of hours and then punched out the headlight on my car when he came back to my house. I wasn't too mad at him because I knew he was heartbroken and disappointed by the news that he wouldn't be a father.

Personally, I was relieved. I didn't even tell him the second time I was pregnant—I miscarried two weeks after the positive pregnancy test. I know now that if either of those babies had lived, I would have been tied to Shane forever.

Everything happens for a reason.

Once again, Shane and I enjoyed a few months of calm and bliss. Things were great until we were hit by the first major tragedy that we had to endure together. We had already lost Shane's grandfather and aunt, but the third death (there were eight in total) involved the first person whose loss I considered to be a devastating tragedy for Shane. In my opinion, this was the death that ignited the fire that would later be the destruction of Shane's mind.

Shane's best friend Joe shot his girlfriend and then himself.

Joe and Shane lived next door to each other growing up, they did everything together, and Shane was crushed when he heard the news. He insisted on attending the funeral completely by himself, and then he disappeared immediately afterward.

And not just for a few hours—Shane vanished for days. His mom and I took turns calling the police, his friends, and his entire family, hoping that someone had heard from him. I drove around the city for hours searching for him with my heart beating rapidly enough to fly out of my chest. We retraced his last moments with his friends at the funeral but didn't get any usable leads.

Due to years of smoking marijuana and deliberately blocking most of my past to preserve my own sanity, I can clearly picture very few moments of my teenage years. The night before we found Shane was certainly one of these memories—for all the wrong reasons.

I was standing in my kitchen, and it was almost midnight. I had thought about trying the hospitals again, but I was scared of what they might tell me. I knew Shane could get out of control if he drank too much—which was going from a rare occurrence to a weekly nightmare—and I wasn't sure what kind of trouble he could get into, being both in an intoxicated state plus depressed over the loss of Joe.

I gave the hospital operator his name, and she asked for his birthday to clarify, since they had multiple Shane Rivards in their system. By that point, I was a wreck and hadn't slept in over 48 hours, so I said my birth year (1979) by mistake. The operator said, "The birthdate of Shane Rivard we have in our system is 1978."—he's one year older than I. Then she immediately asked to put me on hold. The moment the phone went silent, I realized that she had the right year, and my mind started to race uncontrollably, envisioning all sorts of possibilities.

I immediately assumed the worst.

This was before the popularity or affordability of cordless phones, so I was stuck on the phone in the corner of our kitchen. There was no chair close enough, so I lay down on the cool kitchen tile. Light-headedness overtook me, and I didn't even realize that the operator had returned until I heard her say, "We had a Shane Rivard in here almost two years ago, but no one by that name is here now."

I think I hung up without responding. This was the first time I had ever panicked about losing someone, but this was the man I was planning on marrying. I loved Shane, and I wanted to spend the rest of my life by his side. I couldn't handle losing him.

These feelings were a first for me. Due to my turbulent upbringing, I never allowed myself to become too attached to people in my life. I had many friends, but if we fought and the friendship was suddenly over, I moved on without thinking twice about it. I still do so to this day, although I have now developed a few relationships that I doubt I could walk away from without looking back.

After about 64 hours of unexplained wandering, Shane suddenly returned home. The only thing he told me was that he walked around thinking. He snapped at me when I asked, so I never pushed the issue. In fact, we never talked about Joe at all. I tried to a few times, but Shane just got mad. I knew he had just been through so much pain, and I didn't want to force him to talk about it.

I still don't know where he went after the funeral. For all I knew he could have shacked up with some old flame or a random chick he met afterward. I was just relieved he was safe. No matter what happened in our relationship, I always trusted that Shane was faithful.

3

Living with Shane

Shortly after Joe died, Shane and I decided to move in together. I was only nineteen, but my current living situation was suddenly less than ideal. I have to backtrack a bit to explain the drama with my own family during my first two years with Shane.

At the same time I started dating Shane, my mother started dating a recently divorced man, and she was spending an increasing amount of time at his apartment. Around my eighteenth birthday, she decided to move in with him permanently.

The first seven months were every teenager's dream!

Suddenly the freedom I had abused when I was eleven years old was back again, but I was better equipped to handle it. My mother still paid for the house, and she let me live in it by myself. She lost the house when she left my father, and she wanted to keep this home as a safety net. Happily she is still with the same man over fifteen years later, so she never needed to use it.

I loved living there by myself.
All good things must come to an end.

My father had a horrible on-again, off-again relationship with a woman I particularly despised. When my grandmother passed away in the spring, I knew they were not together. There was no mention of them even being together until the middle of the following January, when they announced they would be getting married the next week. I barely saw my father, so I have no idea how long she had been back in his life.

In addition to dropping the marriage bombshell, my father told my brother that he would need to find a new place to live.

The woman he was marrying had two teenage daughters, and she was concerned about having my twenty-one-year-old brother in the house with them. Anyone who knew my brother—which certainly should have included my father—should have immediately known that it would not be an issue.

My brother was truly a good son.

Michael is incredibly smart (basically an overachieving genius like my mother)—a calm, responsible young man, who almost always did the right thing. He will be ashamed if he ever reads this confessional and finds out what his sister was really like growing up.

Michael would have been a good role model for her trouble-making teenage daughters. In fact, I caught her fourteen-year-old daughter sneaking out of the house during the middle of the night—something I could not tattle on since I had done it as well—however, I am willing to bet money that my brother never snuck out of the house once in his life. Michael wasn't perfect, but he also was not a threat to those girls.

My brother was a full-time university student and only worked part-time. He didn't have the financial means to support himself. My father was kicking out the son who had cared for him during his drinking binges and who had stood by his side while he tried to come to terms with my mother's leaving.

The day I moved in with my mother, my brother went from being thirteen years old to thirty years old.

An aunt once said that to me, and it has stuck with me ever since because I know it is so true. I credit Michael with keeping my father alive during those difficult years, and the fact that my father would abandon Michael for this vile woman was disgusting and devastating. It also was heartbreaking to both of us to find out that my father and she were dating again at the same time that we discovered there would be a wedding in a week.

Michael didn't go to their wedding.

I probably shouldn't have gone either. The wedding that I had known about for less than a week involved some incredible planning, including beautiful matching pink bridesmaid dresses worn by the loathsome bride's daughters. It was a lovely, traditional wedding, with all the bells and whistles that you could imagine—not that I remember much of the event in detail.

I drank from the moment I arrived until I stumbled out of the hall just before midnight. My cousins kept track, and they still boast that I had twenty-nine drinks in six hours. They tried to get me to have a thirtieth drink, but I could barely stand up.

It took that many drinks to watch this perfect head table celebrate a blessed union that was essentially excluding my brother and me. When I went to request a father–daughter dance, the DJ questioned whether I really was one of the groom's daughters: "I met the two daughters that are bridesmaids; I didn't know there was a third."

I am his only daughter.

If I hadn't had so much to drink that night, I would have cried. Instead a deep anger built inside me—and it still hasn't subsided. My father has done many other things to upset me since that day, but that was when I realized how unimportant I was in his life.

Despite the late hour, as soon as I got home that night, I called my brother. He was drinking with my mom at her boyfriend's place and still brewing over my dad's shocking choice. I felt ill for my brother, who had sacrificed his social life to care for our father and who then was forced to become even more independent at a time when he should have been focused on his education.

Michael is extremely gifted, and he deserved the opportunity to fully explore his potential. Fortunately, my father's poor decision didn't deter my brother, and Michael finished his degree with honors.

On the other hand, my father's second marriage only lasted about nine months. It ended immediately after his wife stole a huge chunk of his money and gambled it away in Vegas. I felt this behavior was justified, since one of the sore spots in my relationship with my father is his love for money over family.

It disgusts me that he always puts his needs first. My father asks me for favors but never does anything for me in return. Unlike most parents with their children, he blatantly puts his wants ahead of my needs. From what I remember, he didn't start acting this way until my mom had left him. Unfortunately, it is now over twenty-five years later, and I am still having the same arguments with him. In contrast, I can honestly say that I'm always willing to put my stepchildren needs ahead of my own desires, and I have done so for the past nine years.

My father stopped being a dad to me when I was nine years old.

I was not as sympathetic regarding his second failed marriage as I was with the first.

There was an extra room in my mother's house (her old bedroom), and it was immediately decided that Michael would move into her house with me. I love my brother, but we had not lived together—or spent much time together—in the past ten years. I had the place to myself and was accustomed to my carefree lifestyle.

I smoked in the house, had Shane over whenever I wanted, and continued my weekend tradition of hosting little—occasionally big—house parties. I loved my life at that time, and I wasn't thrilled about Michael cramping my style.

My brother was less than thrilled by how I behaved.

As I mentioned, he was always the responsible one and not a typical twenty-one-year-old. He especially hated that I smoked inside the house—although I always tried to hide it—and he was not going to allow the same disrespectful treatment of our mother's home while he lived there. He tried to be my big brother, first by kindly asking me to refrain from smoking and then insisting on it. Finally he complained to my mom—who gave me an ineffective little lecture. Eventually I decided it was time for me to move out. I spent too much of my life doing what I wanted without any interference and I wasn't going to change now that I was practically an adult.

I especially wasn't going to change since I was proud of the woman I was becoming. I had stopped stealing, quit smoking pot, and ended some less-than-beneficial friendships. I also took the initiative of applying at every ad agency, marketing firm, and media-related company in my city. I wrote each one a personalized letter explaining that I wanted to volunteer in order to gain some field experience before I officially enrolled in the program at my local college.

I started volunteering at the first ad agency that offered. Three weeks later, I replaced their bookkeeper-secretary when she suddenly quit. I finally had a real job where I had to dress in heels and a suit. I was proving to myself and to those around me that I had potential and that I would be successful in life.

I thought I was ready to be an adult.

I mentioned earlier that Shane's home situation was borderline unlivable. His circumstances were much worse than mine, so we decided that it only made sense for us to move in together. Fortunately, my mother's new boyfriend knew of an apartment building that needed managing—*everything happens for a reason*—which eliminated the rent aspect altogether.

I was working part-time at the ad agency, and I was waitressing at a golf course on the weekends. I had started working when I was fourteen years old, so I also had a decent savings account. I knew that I made enough money to cover the groceries and utilities, so living with Shane was definitely financially feasible. It honestly seemed like a great idea at the time—despite the facts that we were just starting college and that money would still be extremely tight.

In the beginning, I saw a wonderful side of Shane, one that had faded since the loss of Joe. Shane had renewed energy and inspiration. He joined a new band, played gigs almost every Saturday night, and was really committed to succeeding in school. He was taking a program at the college to get his high-school equivalency diploma, and his grades were pretty good. He had a few part-time jobs here and there, but the majority of the financial responsibilities fell on my shoulders.

The same went for our duties as apartment managers. We did some painting and cleaning together, but I handled all of the rent collection and tenant selection. Both of these tasks ended up being frustrating endeavors due to the area we lived in. Our tenants were thieves and hoarders who were constantly late with the rent. I learned a lot about the rights of tenants and even more about how few rights landlords actually had.

For example, the tenant across the hall had not paid his rent in over two months when the police arrived in the middle of the night, threatening to break down the door. The tenant—a father of three kids—was caught stealing from neighborhood homes, and the police had a warrant to search the apartment. They found enough evidence to place charges, which landed him in jail for the night. Unfortunately, they only kept him one night since the jail was too crowded.

This tenant later made a threat against me, saying that he would punch me in the face if I took his door off its hinges; the threat was on file with the local police, and I included it in my petition to have him legally evicted. However, because I was not allowed to threaten to take the door of its hinges, I got in trouble as well.

I was scolded by the cops and told to pursue eviction through the courts.

When Shane and I finally resigned as mangers several months later, we still had not been able to successfully evict this tenant, and he was then six months behind on his rent. Basically this devious man could do what he wanted, pay nothing for rent, steal anything else he needed, and there were no negative consequences.

Witnessing too many similar situations when I was young and impressionable warped my sense of right and wrong. I could justify anything that I was doing wrong, because I always knew someone else who was worse than I was. This realization also sparks another confession. The time I stole the pack of cigarettes at the hotel was—unfortunately—not the last time I remember stealing something.

Shane and I were always broke. This is not an excuse—just an explanation—but oddly enough, I didn't feel bad about my bad behavior when I was doing it. I feel guiltier and more ashamed about it now. I've done a lot of things in my life that I would never do now, but all of those things were necessary to make me the good person that I've become.

No regrets.

I had little tricks that use to allow me to steal stuff without guilt. Most of the time I was stealing laundry detergent or cases of pop (I am a sick Diet Coke addict to this very day)—my simple trick was to leave the case at the bottom of the cart and hope the cashier didn't notice it. If she did, I simply said, "Oops, I forgot that was there," and then pay for it. I remember only one cashier that noticed the case of pop, and she said, "People forget to mention stuff on the bottom rack all the time."

Maybe I am not the only one who used that trick when money was tight?

Shortly after we moved into our apartment, Shane reunited with his father. After years of barely speaking to Shane, his dad had checked himself into an alcohol rehabilitation program and was sincerely trying to sober up and be a father. Anxious to rebuild their relationship, Shane started visiting him several times a week.

Once his father was able to earn a day pass, he started visiting us at our apartment every Sunday. I would cook a roast or ham, and we would hang out together for hours, chatting as we played darts. When he was sober, Shane's dad was just as charming and loveable as Shane. We had a good life together, and we were sincerely happy.

Shane finally had family in his life, and it made him a better man.
I felt like I was part of a family again, and it renewed my faith in our future.

It was also renewing Shane's commitment to change his life for the better. He was affectionate toward and appreciative of me. He landed a part-time job and kept it for several months, and he even contributed what he could to our expenses. This was the last time our relationship was truly healthy.

Then another of Shane's aunts died, followed by his grandmother on his mom's side, and a cousin that committed suicide. Shane handled these funerals better than Joe's, since he had his father and me by his side. He was a gentle, kind-hearted supporter for his family, and it made me fall in love with him all over again.

Sadly, that changed one sunny afternoon in August.

I remember the weather clearly, because we had been working hard around the apartment and both of us were gross and sweaty from the humidity. I was working about 20 hours a week at each of my two jobs, in addition to managing the apartment building and carrying a full-time college course load. I had no energy to deal with the apartment and was only sleeping four or five hours a night.

All I wanted was a shower and a cold beer on the couch. We recently had decided to leave the apartment building that we were managing and move into a small rental house with my best friend and her boyfriend. We were in the process of cleaning and packing up our apartment when the phone rang.

It was Shane's stepmom. His father was in the hospital.

We dropped everything and rushed to the hospital to find Shane's father on full life support. He had overdosed on one of his medications. Because of the way he had lived, Shane's father always looked significantly older than his fifty years. Now he looked like a frail eighty-year-old man. He was a shell of his former self, and it broke Shane's heart to see him that way.

It broke my heart to see Shane staring at his dad.
His lips trembled, and his eyes filled with tears.
There were no words.

The doctors were not optimistic that Shane's father would ever be able to live without full life support. We spent the next forty-eight hours praying for signs that he might wake, but there was no change. Shane's grand-mother had recently buried her husband, two daughters, and a grand-daughter. Spending hours staring at a hollow version of her youngest child lying lifelessly in front of her was draining what little life she had left in her eighty-seven-year-old body.

The family rallied together to support each other, and they talked about good times they had shared with Shane's dad. There had been countless hospital visits, burial preparations, and funerals in the last few years, so they were ready to push past their tears and accept the inevitable.

Shane was exceptionally quiet and surprisingly optimistic about his father's condition. He showed very little emotion, unless someone suggested that his father's time had come. He was not ready to accept his father's fate, and he argued aggressively with anyone who doubted that his dad was going to be fine.

The first night, we slept—or attempted to sleep—at the hospital in a lounge area. The second night, we went home for a few hours to get a little rest and a much-needed shower. We were wearing the same sweaty clothes from the day before and, after sleeping in them, our scent was unbearable.

I took our time away from the hospital as an opportunity to talk openly with Shane about the chance that his father might not pull through, but I was immediately cut off.

"Shane, I know it is good to stay positive, but the doctors don't feel he will have any quality of life even if he—"

"Even if? Don't say even if! He is going to be okay, and everyone needs to stop acting like he is dying. He will be fine, and I don't want to hear another word about it or I will fucking kill you."

He was squeezing my arm aggressively—like he did during that first incident of physical abuse, when we were on vacation the year before—but this was the first threat against my life. Unfortunately I took it all in context and didn't hold it against him. He was in the process of losing his father, and he was not thinking clearly. Well—that was the logic I used to rationalize Shane's behavior at the time, but I saw evil in his eyes that day.

Something deep inside told me that Shane meant it, but I let it slide.

I had no reason to expect that Shane grabbing me in anger while his father was dying would ever lead to an abusive relationship. He wasn't normally an aggressive kind of guy. He loved to cuddle, opened the door for me, and always behaved like a gentlemen. We once even stopped some guy from abusing a girl in a park. We saw a guy yelling and tossing a girl around, and we both stepped in. Shane was not the kind of guy who would ever be abusive, especially to me. That was how I felt at the time, so I didn't take the first threat seriously.

I stayed quiet for a little while, and then I changed the subject.

We showered, took a nap for a couple hours, had sex, showered again, and went back to the hospital. After another 48 hours of spending most of the day at the hospital, there still was no improvement—in fact, Shane's dad was getting worse—and his family was now openly discussing taking him off life support.

When Shane's aunt was dying of cancer and when his grandfather was in the hospital just before he passed away, Shane's father loudly asserted that life was not worth living if you were stuck in a hospital bed. He was adamant that people were better off passing away peacefully than fighting for what little life they had left.

Shane's father had no life left in him. He couldn't communicate or show any sign that he knew we were there. His lifeless body was hooked up to countless machines. By the end of the fourth day, Shane's stepmom and one of his uncles approached Shane with their decision. They all agreed that taking his dad off life support was for the best, but they wouldn't do it until Shane was ready. Although Shane had five step-siblings (a half-sister on his mom's side and four stepchildren from his dad's second marriage), he was his father's only biological child.

Shane was furious at even the suggestion of turning off the life support.

He screamed and yelled at them for being so cold and inconsiderate. He stormed out of the hospital. I followed him to make sure he was okay and that he didn't do anything too destructive. He was too upset for me to try to explain their position, so I just let him vent. He had a valid point.

He told me that it was not fair that now that he finally had a relationship with his dad, it would be ripped away from him.

He was right—it wasn't fair.
Life is not fair.

I supported Shane's decision that evening and the following day, but on the sixth day his family approached me privately. They convinced me about what I already knew was right, and they begged me to convince Shane. I could see the pain in his grandma's eyes, and I knew she needed to let her son go.

I invited Shane for a walk around the hospital for some fresh air. We were both smokers, so we were constantly going outside, and he didn't seem suspicious that there was anything more to my invite. I kept the conversation light for the first few minutes, and then I suddenly blurted out, "I love you and your dad loves you, but he's gone. He is not living on his terms, and you know he wouldn't want this kind of life if he had a choice. Your family is right."

At first, Shane was upset that I was taking their side, but we walked and talked in circles around the hospital building until he agreed. He was exhausted from fighting the truth. We told his family that he was ready, and they made plans to turn off life support the following day. Until the very last second, Shane remained hopeful that his father would snap out of it—and he sobbed on his father chest once it was finally over.

Everything we had built started to fall apart within a few days of laying his father to rest. This was a critical turning point for Shane. He lost his motivation when Joe died, but he lost his hope of ever having a good life when his father died.

Shane felt all his efforts to improve his life were wasted. He quit his job because they wanted him to go back to work after taking two weeks off—one week while we were in the hospital and one to mourn his father. He started drinking daily, which almost always made him angry and obnoxious. He also started smoking pot again. In fact, I did too.

We were hanging out in his stepmom's backyard a few days after his father's funeral, and his stepbrother offered us a toke. I noticed Shane reached for it without hesitation. I had not smoked any marijuana in over three years.

I also reached for the joint without hesitation.

After three years of not smoking pot, I must admit that it felt incredible. It was so nice to have a break from the stress and reality of our situation. I was sinking deep into debt to keep us afloat, and now Shane had quit another job. I was working two jobs, pursuing a full-time college business program, and living with a very emotionally unstable man. I am not making excuses for my setback. It was easy to slip back into my old ways.

The next three years were the worst years of my life.

4

The Aftermath of Losing Shane's Dad

Shane's personality changed drastically after his dad died. He started to lash out at me over insignificant things. He was constantly picking fights with his friends and family. In my less-than-professional opinion, I think Shane was pushing everyone away intentionally because he couldn't stand the thought of losing someone else he loved.

It worked. Many people in his life stopped spending time with him because they couldn't deal with his anger. Shane became paranoid that the world was against him, and he was determined to fight everyone who questioned his behavior. I was determined to be the one person who stood by him. He needed someone on his side.

Unfortunately, he was trying his hardest to push me away also.
He would say awful and hurtful things to me every time we had an argument.

"You're getting fat like your fat-ass friend."
"Your legs look like nasty cottage cheese."
"Do you really think you should be eating all of that?"

He was right about the fact that I had gained weight. I am a stress eater, and in college I went from 140 pounds to 175 pounds. I actually reached 190 pounds shortly after college when I was only twenty-three years old, but I'll get to that later on. Normally I would lie about my weight, but I promised I would be completely honest in this book, no matter how bad it makes me look. I am proud of myself now and not ashamed of my past. Weight is only a number. It does not define or control me anymore.

I wish my self-esteem had been that strong when I was still with Shane. The negative attacks on my weight caused me to binge eat even more. I would starve myself for as long as I could and then stuff anything I could find in my mouth. I could eat a can of soup, a few handfuls of crackers, a bag of chips, an apple, a chocolate bar, and a massive bowl of popcorn in about an hour. I would just keep grabbing something different until it felt like my belly was going to burst through my skin.

The marijuana I was smoking didn't help.

Weight has always been a sensitive issue for me. It has essentially determined my self-esteem for the majority of my life. Despite being a strong and confident woman, I can feel my self-esteem drop any time the scale goes up. It is a flaw I inherited from my mother, who insisted she was fat even though she could fit into a size two. I've spent most of my life wearing sizes ten and twelve, so I didn't appreciate hearing that she was 'fat' with her tiny size-two waist. She is one of the most attractive women I know, yet she constantly finds flaws in her appearance. I followed suit, and it made my self-esteem an easy target for Shane.

My weight was not the only thing he attacked.

He insulted my cooking, my cleaning, how I dressed, and anything else he could point out to crush my self-esteem. My personality was changing as well. I used to be a confident public-speaker and very outgoing. Even when I was getting into trouble as a preteen, I was never afraid to stand out or speak my mind. I once lip-synced and danced to *I Need a Man* by Annie Lennox in front of my entire high school.

I was fearless before I met Shane.

Now my confidence was shattered, and I was isolating myself from those who loved me. I was starting to believe the horrible things Shane said about me. I felt unattractive, foolish, and ashamed of our relationship. I didn't want the people in my life to see what was really happening.

Too many women let men dictate their self-worth.

Shane repeatedly conned hundreds and thousands of dollars out of me. He lied to me often. He even started to become physically violent. At first, he only squeezed my arm or threw things in my direction, but eventually he started to shove me, spit on me, and grind his palm into my face aggressively. He would get drunk or something would set him off, and he would snap. Mostly he was verbally abusive, but things would turn physical if I dared to say something to defend myself.

When Shane's dad died, we were in the process of moving in with my friend Samantha and her boyfriend. Sadly that situation lasted only a month and half, because of Shane's temper. He got mad at Samantha's boyfriend for using something of his, and he threw a small hammer in the boyfriend's direction. Fortunately the hammer missed hitting him, but it left a big hole in their bedroom door. This time, Shane's behavior cost me a month's rent and my best friend. Samantha decided to move back home, and we couldn't afford the place on our own.

We had to pack up and move again—this time to a tiny apartment just outside of Windsor, in the town of LaSalle. My family moved around a lot when I was young, and this was now the tenth place that I had lived in—and I was only 22 years old. It probably won't come as a shock to any psychiatrist that I do not attach myself to places, property, or material possessions. It is also hard for me to feel attached to any of the people in my life.

Fortunately I am very skilled at making new friends.

Shane was out of control, and he refused counselling no matter how much I begged. I remembered the sweet and loving guy that he had been, and I wanted him back. I kept telling myself that this was just a rough patch.

If I didn't stand by his side, who would?

For over a year, I did my best to maintain the image we were still a healthy and happy couple—until things started to become too bad to hide. Unfortunately, I chose to avoid the people in my life instead of going to them for help. I never confided much in my family or friends until after I left Shane, but deep down I knew I was no longer in a healthy relationship.

For anyone reading this story and wondering why I didn't leave, I don't have an actual answer for you that makes sense to me now. I was a smart and successful woman. We didn't have any kids together. I made the money in the relationship. I thought I was staying because I loved him and because he needed me. I obviously didn't love myself back then since it was so much easier to choose his happiness over my own.

At that time in the relationship, I also had no idea how bad it could get.

Putting on the act that we were happy outside the home was easy compared with acting like I was happy when I was around Shane. He was like a ticking time bomb, and I walked on egg shells trying not to upset him. We could be cuddling on the couch, and a commercial would start a nasty fight. He knew I loved him and that I was willing to put up with the insults and arguments out of pity for the life he had lived.

He took advantage of my love.

Shane's father passed away in August 2001, and the destructive Shane appeared almost immediately after the funeral service. In the beginning, I tolerated Shane's behavior because I sympathized with all the horrible things he had gone through, and I wanted to be the one to save him. I made life at home as easy as possible for him, immediately forgave his outbursts, and basically coddled him to help him keep it together.

The coddling created a monster, because it gave Shane complete control of me.

It was now Father's Day 2002, and we hadn't spoken about his father in months. The subject always brought out the worst in Shane's attitude, so I tried not to bring it up unless it was absolutely necessary. My birthday is in the middle of June, so we had plans to visit my father's side of the family for a birthday-Father's Day family cookout later that day.

Although Shane didn't have many great Father's Day memories with his dad, the previous year's Father's Day was wonderful. Shane and his dad had gone fishing in the Detroit River. They spent the entire day together followed by a barbecue picnic behind our apartment building. I knew attending my family cookout was going to be difficult for Shane. I thought doing something special earlier in the day to honor his dad would make it easier on him.

That was a bad idea.

"Shane, maybe you and I can go fishing together before we go to my dad's, in honor of your dad."

Shane grabbed my throat, squeezed it hard, and said, "If you ever mention my dad again, I will kill you."

The evil that I had seen in Shane's eyes when his father was dying had returned with a vengeance. This was the second time that Shane had threatened my life, and I should have believed him. He loosened his grip and walked away. We didn't even discuss the incident after he calmed down, and he never apologized for it.

I let it slide—again.

Two weeks later, we received a notice in the mail that Shane had an outstanding fine for $5000. He was caught driving without a license and without a valid sticker on his plate. He didn't have either because he was months behind on his car insurance. The law in Canada specifies that you must show proof of insurance to renew your license.

Shane didn't have a job and had worked only a few weeks out of the last year at sporadic part-time jobs or low-paying gigs with his band. I gave him the insurance money each month. I paid our rent, our utilities, our groceries, our gas, and even paid for both of our expensive cigarette habits. My paychecks were stretched so thin that I went $30,000 into debt during the three years that I lived with Shane—and I was making pretty good money at the time.

I was furious, and Shane's only excuse was that he didn't have any 'fun' money. I controlled the money, so he never had any extra cash to do things with his friends. He was using the insurance money to enjoy his life, since life was short, and he wanted to live his before it was gone. I respect the concept and try to live my life that way now, but that doesn't mean I should allow someone else to live off my hard work. If you want to enjoy your life to the fullest, you need to be able to cover your own expenses.

I ended up paying a lawyer $1500 to reduce the fine to $1000. This time, I made Shane show me the receipt from the lawyer, since I couldn't leave work to go to the hearing. I was worried we would receive a bill in the mail a few weeks later stating that we still owed the lawyer.

He conned me out of another $1000 two months later.

I was thinking of starting my own home-based advertising agency. I had worked at one for almost three years while I was in college, and I had been selling advertising space for the past year. Many of my clients wanted additional advertising services that the business I currently worked for didn't handle.

Shane told me he found a deal on a great computer and desk for $1000. He said the computer was less than a year old and that it came with a printer. It was something I needed, and the price seemed fair. Unfortunately, on the day that Shane brought it home, there was only a desk.

He claimed the guy tricked him. I argued every side of it and insisted that he return the desk and get my money back. He kept saying that he couldn't get it back because the guy who sold it to him was nowhere to be found.

I still don't know the truth about what happened to the computer I was supposed to get, but that was the last time I gave Shane money directly. I would pay for anything he needed, but I wouldn't hand him cash. I told him he needed to get a job and that he had to start contributing to the home. It was about a year since his father died, and it was time to put his life back together.

He made an attempt.

Shane decided he wasn't ready to go back to college, so he found a job through an employment agency. He started work at his new job on a Monday and quit on a Wednesday. The boss was impossible, and the company treated their employees horribly. The employment agency set him up with a new job.

He started work at his new job on a Monday and quit on a Wednesday. The boss was impossible, and the company treated their employees horribly. The employment agency set him up with a new job.

He started work at his new job on a Monday and quit on a Wednesday. The boss was impossible, and the company treated their employees horribly. The employment agency set him up with a new job.

I intentionally copied and pasted those same three sentences three different times. Shane did have three jobs in three weeks, all thanks to the temp agency. He started each job on a Monday and quit each one on the Wednesday. After the third week, the employment agency decided not to find him another job. They knew he wasn't worth their time.

I should have known the same thing.

This was the first time I really had the guts to stand up to him. I'd yelled back at him, argued with him, but I had never really stood up for myself. I always caved. Every time we fought, Shane got his way, and all was forgiven. Any woman who has been emotionally and mentally abused can understand just how easy it is to be controlled when you love someone unconditionally.

I had been with this man for six years. He was my life.

I was his only source of support. He had a selfish and destructive mother, his father was gone, and his best friend took his own life. He needed me, and I was willing to make any sacrifice necessary to keep him alive and well.

But every woman needs to put a limit on what she will endure.

After Shane quit his third job in three weeks, he took the money he had earned and bought himself a PlayStation 2. Yes, he actually did that. I was furious. I was paying for groceries on my credit card, and he had just spent $300 on a video console. What was even worse is that I asked him to return it, and he refused.

So, I did something completely out of character.

I found the receipt and returned the game system myself. I told the clerk at Wal-Mart that I was returning it because my boyfriend was an idiot. I took the money he spent on it and I used all of it toward our rent and food. I knew Shane would be less than thrilled by my sudden backbone, but I needed to make a stand or he would continue using me for as long as I'd let him. I spent every cent of the money, and I didn't say anything to him until the following day.

I waited for him to notice that the PlayStation 2 was gone.

"Where's the PlayStation 2?"

"At Wal-Mart."

"Funny—where did you put it?"

"I said we couldn't afford it. I told you that we needed money for groceries, so I took the receipt and returned it. That's why we have food in our fridge now."

"You better not be serious!"

I was expecting him to be upset, but I wasn't expecting just how upset he would be.

Maybe I should have expected it, but this was the first time he forcefully ground his palm into my face, and I had no idea how much it could hurt. He had grabbed my face before, but this time he was really mad.

Shane's physical abuse toward me had grown gradually, and it wasn't really bad until near the end. As much as Shane would throw and break stuff, he never did anything more than squeeze my arm aggressively until his father passed away. Then each time was a little more painful than the previous incident.

It all started with a rough arm squeeze that I never should have forgiven.

Abuse always gets worse.

Once you've allowed an abuser to treat you that way, he or she will keep testing the limits to see how much you'll take before you fight back. When this particular act of physical aggressiveness first started, Shane just squeezed my face. He put his hand on my face, extended his fingers, and pressed inward. It hurt a little at first, but his actions were more forceful each time it happened.

On the day that he discovered that his PlayStation 2 was missing, it was the angry, crazed look in his eyes that really bothered me. We were in our tiny apartment, standing where the kitchen opened into the living room. He pressed his palm into my face, and then he used his hand to push me backward toward our couch as he screamed, "Get it back now!"

He had my head pinned into the couch cushion. I could feel his fingertips indenting the edges of my face. His palm was covering most of my mouth, but I could still breathe. He held it there for a minute or two before letting me go and standing up.

"I can't. The money is already spent."

"Buy a new one. You owe me a PlayStation!"

"Well, you owe me about $20,000, so I'll buy you one when you pay me back for the lawyer, the car insurance, a year's worth of rent and groceries, and the computer I paid you for but never received."

I was shocked that I had the guts to say all this after being pinned to the back of the loveseat, but it felt good to stand up for myself.

Apparently I was stepping over the line by pointing out the obvious. Shane grabbed the closest thing to him—the remote control—and wheeled it at my head. It missed. He then grabbed our lamp and threw it at a wall. When I screamed at him to stop, he grabbed a jar of jam off the kitchen table and threw it at the hutch that my grandfather had built. He knocked off two wine glasses, which shattered into countless tiny pieces.

I grabbed my purse and said I was leaving him.

He said, "Good, get lost."

I am not sure if this is when I developed my habit of driving around with the radio cranked to clear my head, but I remember doing it when I left the apartment on that cool September afternoon. From our little apartment in LaSalle, you could drive along the waterfront on an uninterrupted path to the town of Tecumseh, which was about twenty-five kilometers away. It took me almost an hour to go as far as I could along the water before I needed to turn around. This has always been my favorite route and I've traveled it often—in both good times and bad.

During this particular drive, I discovered that I could rationalize Shane's behavior and make myself into the bad guy. I started off singing songs like Gloria Gaynor's *I Will Survive* and finished the drive singing *Stay* by Lisa Loeb. I convinced myself that I was being too hard on him. He was going through a rough time, and it was unfair of me to sell the video console he bought without telling him first. I pulled back into the driveway to our little apartment in LaSalle ready to make up and put this recent incident behind us.

Unfortunately, his car was gone. I went inside and noticed that the mess from earlier was still there. I picked up the lamp and the broken glass and scrubbed the jam off the hutch and rug. The hutch was in our kitchen, but the apartment was so old and cheap that it had rough, navy blue industrial carpet in the kitchen. It was actually the same carpet that was in the tiny office, living room, and bedroom.

After I put the house back together, I lit a cigarette on the two-foot-by-two-foot porch that was just outside our apartment. I chain-smoked cigarettes and weed for an hour as I waited for him to come home.

The fight had happened before I had made us dinner, so when I realized that I had barely eaten anything that day, I went inside to find a snack. Our below-the-poverty-line lifestyle meant there wasn't much food in the house, but I polished off a whole sleeve of saltine crackers with about half a dozen cheese slices.

I turned on the TV but didn't really watch anything in particular. I listened to music, I called my friends and talked about everything except my fight with Shane, and I ate anything I could scrounge up. I couldn't confide in my friends about what was going on, because I was certain they would convince me to leave him. Food was my favorite friend because it didn't judge.

Hours went by, and it was after midnight. Shane didn't call, and he didn't come home.

Eventually I feel asleep alone on the couch. Around 5:00 am, I woke up to him coming home— drunk and seconds away from passing out. I let him sleep and waited until the morning to discuss what had happened.

I was lying in bed the following morning pretending that I was sleeping. I was dreading the conversation that I was going to have when Shane finally woke up, but we never actually discussed the incident. He kissed my cheek as soon as he woke up and simply acted as if nothing had happened. I foolishly went along with the façade that everything was fine.

It was easier to ignore what was happening to our relationship than it was to deal with it.

Shane was always sweet and charming when he was sober. He suggested going out for breakfast together (even though it was almost noon), but I told him we couldn't afford it, and I made us soup and grilled cheese instead. I wasn't sure if I should wreck the unusually calm moment by asking where he was last night until 5:00 am.

After we ate, he realized that he lost his expensive Oakley sunglasses during his drunken debauchery. The previous winter, he had used his birthday and Christmas money to buy a pair of $260 sunglasses—despite my disapproval. My sunglasses cost $10, and I didn't think it was responsible for the guy without a job to spend such an obscene amount of money on brand-name eyewear.

My opinion didn't matter to him.

Shane confessed that he slept in a parking lot downtown for a few hours after leaving the bar, so we drove there to look for his sunglasses. He remembered exactly where he had lain down, so we found them after only a few minutes of searching. Unfortunately they were considerably damaged. Eight months later, I found out how he really lost them in the parking lot, but I'll explain those embarrassing details later on.

Not everything in our relationship was bad. Although I lost my self-esteem somewhere along our journey together, I wouldn't have stayed with Shane so long if there weren't still some good times. I've been highlighting the bad memories, but there were some wonderful moments as well.

I remember a fantastic trip when we went white water rafting in Ottawa with his stepmom and family.

His stepmom paid for the trip, since we obviously couldn't afford it on our own. I was nervous about going, because Shane was still not comfortable discussing his father. I thought that his temper was going to appear at a few different points during the five days we were away, but nothing bad actually happened. He was enjoying time with his family, which was exceptionally surprising since he had never been close to that side of his family—or any family.

After the trip, Shane found a new full-time job, and things settled down for a few short weeks. He reunited with some friends from college and started to talk about going back to school in January. He also started treating me significantly better. He showed his appreciation for everything I did for him and even complimented me on a few occasions.

I now have a theory about relationships that involves a grading scale. I use it for my personal and professional relationships, so I don't find myself in a bad situation again. The people in my life need to maintain a passing grade (D- or higher) to stay in my life. To me that means the relationship needs to be happy and mutually beneficial at least 50% of the time. I also won't tolerate any form of abuse, but that should be every person's rule.

I now choose to spend most of my time with people who have earned As.

Every relationship is going to experience bad patches, but that doesn't mean the relationship is a waste of time. It is still important to be supportive of the people who matter in your life when they are going through difficult times. As long as the good outweighs the bad, the relationship is still worth saving. At this point in my life with Shane, the relationship was still good 60%-70% of the time.

We had issues, but we still enjoyed each other's company and shared many special moments together. Regardless of the good times, I should have already left him. The physical aggression and death threats were more than I should have allowed. That behavior should have given him an automatic F, but I didn't value myself back then the same way I do today.

The first time a man lays his hands on a woman aggressively should be the last time he ever puts his hands on her. In her heart, every woman knows that she should walk away immediately, yet most willingly stay with their abusers. My mistake was in focusing too much on the good in Shane and the happy memories we shared.

Sadly the happiness we felt when we got back from our trip was also short-lived.

When Shane was at the college getting his high-school equivalency diploma, he had a favorite teacher—Gary Stewart. Gary went by the nickname Stew and quickly became 'one of the guys.' Shane and three of his buddies from college played euchre and weekend Risk tournaments with Stew. Despite the fact that he was about thirty years older than they were, Stew partied all night long with the rest of the college kids.

After a night of drinking too much with the college boys, Stew had a fatal heart attack. He had become Shane's father figure, and now he was gone too. I knew the moment Shane heard the news that Stew was gone that this would be one death too many. Shane was still not over losing his dad, and now—just fourteen months later—he was burying the next closest thing to a father.

5

After Stew Passed Away

I had some hope in the beginning, because Stew's death appeared to bring Shane and his friends closer together, but this closeness was short-lived. The Saturday after the funeral, all the guys were supposed to celebrate Stew's life with some drinking, cards, and possibly a game of Risk at Dave's house.

I received a call around 11:00 pm from Dave, asking me to pick up Shane.

"Shane's out of control and pissing everyone off. You need to get him before something bad happens."

I hate to admit it, but that was not the first time I picked up Shane because he was misbehaving, but I didn't expect it to end as badly as it did. A few months earlier, I had picked up Shane from jail after a bout of public drunkenness, and that night was easy compared to what I was about to experience.

The party was at Dave's house, which was by the college and only about ten minutes from our house. I was met in the driveway by Dave and his girlfriend, who immediately started to tell me all the horrible things Shane had done and said. He was arguing with his friends about everything. He was also throwing and breaking things in their house.

Shane threw a temper tantrum the second that he saw me standing outside talking to our mutual friends.

"What the fuck is she doing here?"
"Dave asked me to come. It's time to go home."
"I'm not going anywhere. Get lost! Why do you have to ruin everything?"
His friends helped me coax him in the car as he screamed and swore at all of them. We headed home. He ranted, and I drove in silence. I was particularly upset because I noticed a few girls at the party, and Shane had promised it was guys-only. Shane told me that was why I wasn't invited.

Many of the people whom I saw at the party were actually friends of mine as well. If I had been there with him, I could have helped to keep him under control. I had plenty of experience helping Shane stay calm while he was drinking. Most of our uglier fights happened on nights where I didn't arrive on the scene until after he had already lost control.

It was late when we got home, so I immediately went to bed. I hid both sets of car keys under the mattress and shut the door to our room. He was still angry and ranting about how he hated everyone. I told him that he needed to settle down and go to sleep. I went to bed without even trying to discuss what had just happened, since I knew he was in no shape to talk about it rationally.

I was smart enough not to start a fight with Shane when he was already angry and drunk.

I was just starting to fall asleep when I heard him come in the room. I lay still, so I didn't have to talk to him. I was lying on my left side, facing the bedroom door, but I kept my eyes closed. I didn't hear him approach me; I just felt him throw himself on top of me. He pushed me onto my back and grabbed the pillow from his side of the bed. He quickly forced the pillow over my face. He was straddling my body as he tried to smoother me with it, but fortunately I was able to turn my head to one side.

He started screaming over and over again, "You made me kill my father."

It took me a second to realize what was happening, and then—surprisingly—my instincts kicked in. I was able to bring my knee into his groin and apply some pressure to his scrotum. It was enough pain to cause him to pull away from me and sit up straight. He was no longer pressing down on my chest, and the pillow was now an inch or two above my face.

I could tell he was losing his balance and his hold on me. I quickly pushed my upper body into his chest. He was stunned that I was fighting back, which gave me the opportunity to toss him off of the bed and onto the floor before he could even react.

He had a crazed look in his eye, but so did I.

I started kicking and screaming, pushing him out of our bedroom door. I think he snapped out of whatever had overcome him, because he didn't put up much of a fight. He must have been shocked to see me that way. I didn't usually fight back. I shut the door to our room and then slid our dresser in front of the door. I piled everything heavy I could on top of the dresser and then flopped onto the bed, crying uncontrollably.

What just happened?
How did we get here?

This was the first time that I could have died, and I'm proud that I fought to save my life. I still valued my life at that point. I honestly value my life now, but there was a dark period in between when I forgot how much I had to offer the world.

I never went to sleep that night. I could not stop crying long enough to catch my breath. My sobbing was drowned out by the insanely loud television that was blaring in our living room. Shane knew how much I hated hearing a loud TV when I was trying to fall asleep.

It was early in the morning when I gave up on sleeping and started preparing for how I was going to handle this situation. I got dressed and packed a small bag with all the essentials. I moved the weighted-down dresser away from the door, and I went into the living room. Shane was passed out in our reclining loveseat. Our apartment wasn't big enough to fit a full-sized sofa.

I was careful not to wake him up.

I wrote a quick letter telling him that I couldn't take it anymore. I said I would be going out for a few hours and that I would appreciate if he wasn't there when I got back. I would find somewhere else to live, and we could work out the details once I had the chance to clear my head.

I was finally ready to put an end to his abuse.

I tossed my bag in the backseat and drove down Riverside Drive. I went from LaSalle, through Windsor, to Tecumseh, and then a few miles farther into Belle River. An hour had passed, but I wasn't ready to go back. I played loud music, chained smoked, and cried. Finally I decided to pull over in a parking lot to write. I am a writer, so I always keep a pen and paper in my car.

Inspiration can happen at any moment.

I mostly wrote short poems or potential song lyrics. All of which were either morbidly depressing or surprisingly motivational. I was ready to end this chapter of my life. It had gone too far, and I deserved better. After three hours, I finally felt ready to go home.

Shane's car was still in the parking lot of our apartment building. I grabbed a coffee from the Tim Horton's across the street and kept on driving. I smoked two more cigarettes and headed back to the apartment. Shane's car was still there.

This time I pulled in and parked alongside his car. I was ready to stick up for myself. Helping him was not worth risking my life, and it was time to lay down the law. When I got inside, Shane immediately turned off the TV and stared at me with his kindest baby-blue eyes.

"I am so sorry. I don't remember all the details, but I know I was an ass yesterday, and I feel horrible."

"Not good enough."

"Losing Stew was just too much. I drank too much. I blacked out and don't even remember anything after we left Dave's, and yes, I know I need to apologize to them too."

"You tried to fucking kill me."

"What!"

"You jumped on me and put a pillow over my face."

"I did not. I couldn't. Is that why I was locked out of our room?"

"Yes! You jumped on me and tried to smoother me with a pillow. I kicked you in the balls, tossed you out of the room, and spent the rest of the night crying. It's too much; I can't handle it anymore."

"Honestly, I would never want to hurt you. I love you. I blacked out."

"You scared the shit out of me. You could have killed me."

"I could never kill you."

Shane sat back down on the couch and started to cry. I sat down next to him. We hugged and then held each other. He looked and sounded so sincerely sorry. I could tell that he wasn't in control of his actions, so I used this opportunity to suggest once again that he seek help.

"Shane, you need to talk to someone."

He said he would get help, but he never did. I made him appointments and left brochures on the kitchen table, but I couldn't force him to go. He kept coming up with excuses to put it off. I didn't move out either. Instead I lived in fear of what might happen next. I avoided him, smoked a lot of marijuana, and just prayed things would eventually go back to normal. Things calmed down for about a month, but I could tell he still wasn't really himself. He was paranoid, distant, and moody.

The next major incident was just after Christmas.

His band was playing a gig downtown. He said he would call me when it was over to come pick him up. He didn't want me at the gig, and I foolishly agreed. I was overweight—over 180 pounds by this point—and severely depressed. I didn't mind staying home, getting high, and pigging out while I waited for his call.

I was spending more and more time hiding in our apartment.

56

It was a half-hour drive to the bar, so he always called the moment a gig was over. The gig was done at 2:00 am, and he still hadn't called by 2:30 am. Finally, at 3:00 am I left for the bar to find out what was going on. When I arrived to pick him up, there was an older and unattractive woman sitting on his lap. Shane looked drunk and smug. I was not in the mood for another horrible night of unpredictable behavior, so I tried to stay calm.

It was hard to stay calm.

"Shane, grab your gear; it's time to go."
"I'm having fun."
"I don't care. I'm your ride, and I am ready to go."
"You go, and I'll stay."
"The bar is closed, you have some ugly whore on your lap, and you are about to lose the best thing in your life. Get up and let's go."
"Fuck you, just go."

I should have turned around and left, but he had hundreds of dollars' worth of equipment that needed to be packed up, and I didn't want him to leave it all behind. I could tell he was too drunk to take care of it on his own, and I didn't want him making a mistake he would regret later on—such as sleeping with that nasty old woman and ruining our relationship forever.

So I packed up all of his equipment completely by myself.

He watched me go up and down the stairs, carrying his heavy gear, as he loudly flirted with the unattractive groupie. After I secured all of his equipment, I demanded that he get in the car with it. He argued and complained for at least ten minutes, but eventually—with the help of his band members—he got in.

Shane's friends told me later on that they always felt sorry for me. They saw what I put up with from Shane and knew I deserved better. I wish one of them would have told me that when I was still with him.

I'm not sure why I didn't see it. I was a strong, determined woman when I met Shane.

Why I was so desperate to save such a horrible relationship?

Shane had not treated me right for the past few years, yet I wouldn't leave the bar without him, because I didn't want him sleeping with some random woman and ruining our relationship. In hindsight, our relationship was already ruined. The person I am today would have ended our destructive relationship long before it ever got to this point.

On the ride home, Shane wanted to stop at a local restaurant for chicken wings. It was almost 4:00 am, and the place was obviously closed. I told him that it was closed, but he was certain he was right. He insisted that I drive by the place just to check if it was open. It was about 15 minutes out of our way, and I was exhausted—but I still did it.

I wanted to prove that it was closed, so he would shut up about it.

"See, it's closed."
"Stop, I think it's open."
As he said that, he slammed my brand-new car into park while I was going about fifty kilometers per hour (about thirty miles per hour). I had a horrible history of bad cars, and this was the first time I had a decent vehicle. Fortunately, he didn't do any damage to this car.

Shane never respected my property, and that reason alone should have been enough for me to leave him. In the history of our relationship, Shane punched in one of my headlights, kicked a dent in the side of my door, and tore off my rear-view mirror, which he then tossed out the car window as I was driving down the expressway. He also peed out my car window while I was driving him home from the bar on at least two occasions that I can remember.

Why I was so desperate to save such a horrible relationship?

That question is worth repeating, because if I am fortunate enough to publish this book (which I will be since *positive thinking brings positive results*), then I know there will be countless women reading it, and too many of those women know in their hearts that they should be asking themselves that very same question.

Why do so many people—women especially—stay in abusive relationships?
I still don't know the answer, but I know I will never put myself through that again.
I deserve better.

Unfortunately Shane's bad behavior at the bar and slamming my car into park wasn't the end of this particular story. Once he realized that he couldn't get his chicken wings, he started complaining about how hungry he was and that we never had any good food at home. I should have responded that we would have better food in the apartment if he could keep a job, but I was trying to maintain the peace. I was scared of what he might do if I upset him.

This was before I realized that I deserved better.

I stopped at a store and bought a few bags of chips, just so he would have something to shove in his mouth. I didn't have to listen to him if his mouth was full of food. Unfortunately, when we got back to the apartment, he opened one of the bags, turned it upside down, and dumped all the chips onto our carpeted kitchen floor. He then stomped on them while whining that he really wanted chicken wings. It was like watching a two-year-old child throw a tantrum.

Now that Shane, his guitar, and amps were safe at home, my patience gave out.

"I am sick of babysitting you. Clean up the chips and go to bed. I am done dealing with you."

As I stormed past him, he threw a coffee mug at me. It whizzed by my ear and busted the ceramic handle on one of our kitchen cabinets. I grabbed a knife and the car keys before going into our bedroom. I tucked them all under the mattress and moved the dresser back in front of our bedroom door before he had a chance to follow me. He stayed in the living room with the TV blaring loudly all night long.

Even before he tried to smother me, I slept better when Shane was not in the bed.

At some point in our relationship, I stopped caring about my own health and happiness. I have always hated listening to a TV when I am trying to sleep. I need the room to be dark and quiet. Shane needed to watch TV, or he couldn't fall asleep. When we were first together, he used to keep the volume really low and put the sleep-time function on the TV, so that it would turn off after an hour. I would wait for him to fall asleep, and then I would fall asleep.

After his dad passed away, Shane struggled to fall sleep, so he would keep the TV on all night. He also would get extremely angry with me and put the volume up louder if I tossed and turned while he was trying to sleep. He accused me of intentionally moving around just to keep him awake.

"Every time I start to fall asleep, you roll your huge ass over and shake the whole bed. I think you are doing it on purpose."

Shane accused me a few times of doing things to drive him crazy, but in reality I was doing everything I could to stop him from going crazy on me. I am embarrassed to admit this now, but I would even apologize for moving in bed and then lay as perfectly still as possible until he fell asleep. I was afraid to cough, twitch, or turn when he was lying next to me.

I always slept better without him.

Shane had another gig the following night. He tried acting sweet and innocent in the morning, but I ignored him. He knew he had messed up again. Nothing was actually said about his behavior the night before, but at least this time, he did clean up the mess that he had made with the chips. I avoided him most of the day by running errands, and I refused to cook him any meals. I made sure to make only enough food for myself. He tried to kiss me goodbye before he left for his gig, but I walked away. I was fed up and not sure what I was going to do next.

Timing is everything.
Up until this point, I had kept my house tidy.

It is an analogy I make with how my mother and I—probably most women—handle life when things get messy. My mom was a teenage bride and mother of two, but her house was always spotless. She went through tough times, financial struggles, and being treated poorly by various people in her life, but no one ever knew her pain. She always maintained the appearance that everything was okay. Unfortunately, I inherited that trait, and my silence almost killed me.

When I was a troublesome teenager, I kept up appearances.

No one knew how bad I was really being, because I kept my 'house' tidy. I always received good grades in school, I had respectable friends, and I had a good part-time job. The same is true of the time I spent with Shane. We always acted like a happy, normal couple around other people. I always spoke highly of him. I dressed well and had a professional job, and no one knew my house was not in order. I always kept it tidy.

I couldn't hide the mess any longer.

I was finally at my breaking point, and I really needed to confide in my friends, but no one was home. I had just recently lost one of my closest friends because she betrayed me. I was selling advertising space for a local business magazine, and I got her a job selling ads for the LaSalle newspaper. She did really well in the beginning, but then she got pregnant with her third child.

She started forging contracts to fill the ad space. She was signing renewal forms for former clients without asking them if they wanted to continue. Once she went on maternity leave, these businesses started to complain that they were being charged for ads they didn't approve. There was over $4000 in forged contracts, for which she had already been paid commission.

When I asked her if it was true, she assured me she did not forge anything and that it was all a misunderstanding. She promised me, so I loudly and proudly defended her to everyone at work. I trusted her completely. After two weeks of investigation, the evidence was undeniable. She called my boss so she could confess, and then she called me.

"Are you stoned?"

"No, why?"

"I have something to tell you, and it might be better if you were stoned."

So, I smoked a joint while I listened as she confessed.

I was furious. My boss called me into his office the next day and told me about their conversation. He said that she swore I knew nothing about it (which I didn't), and he wanted to get my thoughts on the situation. I told him that she just lost the best friend she ever had—me—which was true.

Despite my boss believing in my innocence, my coworkers took it upon themselves to persecute me for the crime. They made working there unbearable to the extent that I was vomiting before work each day—although some of that was to do with the stress I was hiding in my home life. One of the women in my office even keyed my new car. I was the leading salesperson, and I think they were jealous of my success. They wanted to use this scandal to get rid of me.

The other friends I had at that time were all on vacation. One was on a cruise with her family, one was up north visiting her family for Christmas, and the other was on vacation with her family at a ski resort. They all had exciting plans—with their families. I barely spoke with my family. I was still angry at my parents for their mistakes during my upbringing, plus I was embarrassed to be around anyone because of how my life was now falling apart. It was the week between Christmas and New Year's Eve, and I was all alone.

I felt very alone.

I chained smoked, I drank several of Shane's beers, and I got high. I stuffed my face with any food that I could find in our cupboards and listened to the most depressing music. I was crying so hard that I couldn't catch my breath, which—combined with the alcohol—was making me feel dizzy and nauseated.

I finally had enough self-destruction. I wanted a more permanent solution.

I didn't feel like I would ever be strong enough to leave Shane, and I couldn't stay in this relationship much longer. I was in so much debt, my job was horrible, and my family support system was almost nonexistent. All of my attempts to improve my life were spoiled by reality.

I wrote a short and sweet goodbye letter.
It wasn't just a goodbye letter to Shane. I was ready to leave everyone.

> Shane–
> I've had enough. I can't watch you self-destruct anymore. You won't get help, and I'm now afraid of you. This relationship will never be good again. You use me, and you don't appreciate anything I have done to help you. I can't save you. I give up.
> Please pass along the following message to my family and friends:
> Don't worry–I've made peace with this decision. I made a mess of this life, and I can't fix it now. Hopefully, I'll be given a chance at a new life. Don't grieve for me. I am in a better place. Love always.

I believed in reincarnation at that time in my life, and I wasn't afraid of dying. I wanted Shane to feel guilty about how he had treated me, but I didn't want my family and friends to be hurt by my decision. I thought my note would help ease my family's grief and act as a wake-up call for Shane.

In reality, I had that backwards. My family and friends would have been crushed.

Shane was already too far gone to be affected by it.

I remember exactly how I felt at that moment. I felt overwhelmed by the destructive relationship, by debt, and by the drama at work. I felt unattractive and overweight. I was mad at myself for my past mistakes and thought it would be impossible to ever have a good life. I wanted a chance to start over, and I felt that dying was the only option I had.

I downed a small souvenir bottle of tequila with a slimy caterpillar in the bottom of it. My brother had given it to me three years earlier, when he came back from a trip to Mexico. It tasted absolutely disgusting. Without putting on shoes or a coat, I went outside.

I walked in my socks through the two-inch-thick snow in the long, neglected yard behind the apartment building. The backyard ended when it reached the Detroit River. I stood on the edge of the yard for almost an hour. I was freezing as I gazed at the huge body of water in front of me, but my body didn't tremble. My feet felt like heavy bricks of ice, but I didn't actually feel cold.

I was physically frozen in time.

I was trying to get enough courage to dive in. I wanted to swim to the bottom and then float away. I was not afraid of drowning. I was more worried that my natural instinct would kick in, and I would fight to survive. I didn't want to be known as some pathetic person who attempted suicide. I already felt like I had failed at life—I didn't want to also fail at dying.

I wanted a real and permanent escape from my life.

All I needed to do was jump in the water and swim to the bottom.

I would be free from Shane, free from my massive debt, free from my stressful job, and I could sleep peacefully at the bottom of the river.

The longer I stood there, the more I thought about all the good there was inside of me. I was smart, compassionate, hard-working, and I was loved by most people who knew me. I wanted to punish Shane for his behavior by losing me, but in reality, that meant I would be gone, forever. I was afraid I would fight to live because deep down I knew I deserved to live.

I once had so much potential.

I also worried about how Shane would handle losing me. He already had lost so many of the key players in his life that I felt the death of me would push him over the edge—if he wasn't there already. I was angry with him, but I knew that the death of me would end up being the death of Shane as well.

As much as I wanted to end it all, I couldn't bring myself to jump in the river. Thank God.

I finally went inside and decided that I was going to start fresh tomorrow. Shane could find his own way home—if he even planned on coming home at all. I popped a few too many Tylenol and went to bed with a newfound determination. If the alcohol and pills didn't kill me, then I was meant to live, and I was going to start living life on my own terms.

I left the letter on the dresser just in case I didn't make it through the night.

Shane finally came home a few hours later. He must have taken a cab home, and he seemed somewhat sober. He kissed me on the cheek as I pretended to be asleep. He went to sleep without turning on the TV, which was a strong sign that he was trying to be considerate of my feelings. He didn't see the letter on the dresser.

The next day I laid down the law, and he agreed that he was ready to make some changes.

"From now on you need a part-time job. You need to start contributing at least $100 per week to our expenses. You will only drink once a month, and I need to be there. If you get violent or crazy again, I am gone, and I won't come back. You also will find a counselor. I don't care what it costs, you need help, and I will not tolerate any more excuses."

I meant it at the time, but three days later, it was New Year's Eve, and Shane was an ass again. We went to my friend's house together to celebrate the New Year and our fresh start. I said he could drink, but instead he snorted some cocaine behind my back and then he lost all control. He even peed on my friend's living room carpet.

I wanted to curl up into a ball and die. He embarrassed me for the last time that night, and I went from being understanding and sympathetic to feeling like I could literally kill him. It was certainly embarrassing enough that I should have ended our relationship over it.

I thought leaving him would essentially kill him.

I didn't leave Shane the next day like I should have, but I started bossing him around, and treating him as poorly as he has treated me. There was no sex, no cooking for him, and I only bought groceries that I wanted.

I told Shane that he was going to learn what it was like to live without my help, because that was where our relationship was headed if he kept up the destructive behavior. I thought this threat might inspire him to take control of his life again.

It didn't.

The lack of sex and good food was making him miserable and harder to be around. All we did was fight. Three weeks later, there was another inexcusable incident where he pushed me aggressively off our porch. He gave me a shove from behind, and my feet slipped out from under me. There were only six stairs, and my tailbone landed on the middle step. I came very close to smashing my head on the concrete porch, but my puffy ponytail gave me just enough of a cushion to protect my skull.

The fight was over his birthday gift.

He wanted a $35-a-month year-long membership at a large fitness chain. Instead I decided to buy him a $100-per-year membership at a small gym next to our apartment building. It had cardio equipment and weights, plus a variety of strength-training classes. It was all I could afford.

Shane actually asked me to get memberships for both of us, since he was now starting to gain weight as well, and he didn't want us to become one of those 'fat couples.' He also told me that he would be happier and nicer to me if I looked like I did when we first started dating.

Ouch.

Shane saw me coming out of the less-expensive gym, accused me of meeting a guy in there, and then got even more upset when I told him the truth. He called me a cheap, selfish bitch and told me to return the worthless membership and get him one at a real gym. I was trying to get away from him because he was yelling at me erratically, but he followed me outside.

That was when he pushed me off the porch.

Once he realized I was hurt, he immediately helped me back up, and I followed him inside with his arm around my waist. He walked me to our bedroom. I slid into the bed, hid under the comforter, and cried for hours. My back hurt, but that wasn't why I was crying. Shane left the house a few minutes later without saying where he was going.

I allowed him to do what he wanted without any consequences.

Shane seemed drunk when we were arguing about the gym membership, but it was mid-afternoon, and I hadn't seen him drinking all day. He only left the house for about an hour, which is when I snuck over to the gym. It wasn't until a few months later that I realized he had a coke habit and that he was probably high when we had this ridiculous argument.

His cocaine habit also explained all the money he stole or conned from me. I don't know when or how it began, but I heard a few stories from his friends that he snorted it when I wasn't around. I've never touched it and never would.

The idea of snorting a chemical substance scares me more than Shane did.

Shane couldn't have been doing coke every day, because he still had some profound moments of clarity. The next day, Shane was the responsible one who finally took control of the problem. I was crying on the couch and asking him what it would take to get us back to the way we used to be, when he came up with the solution.

"You need to leave me. You keep saying it, but you don't. You forgive me instead, and I am going to keep treating you like shit because you let me. You need to leave me before I really hurt you."

That was the greatest thing he could have done for me. In the past, he always begged me to stay—and I had never needed much convincing. This time, he knew that I needed to go before it got worse, but he also recognized that I didn't have the strength to make that difficult decision on my own.

I was too worried about whether he would survive without me that I was neglecting to consider whether I would survive being with him. Despite all the horrible stories I've shared about Shane, there was a reason I still had hope things would get better for us. Shane was a good guy deep inside. He didn't truly want to hurt me.

Shane gave me a way out—and I took it.

I moved in with my father, which was a shocking choice given our relationship. For numerous reasons, my father and I were not—and are not—close. Unfortunately, I wasn't comfortable moving in with my mother and her boyfriend, and none of my friends had a spare room. In fact, most of my friends were still smart enough to live at home since we had just recently graduated college or university. I couldn't afford a place of my own because I needed to get caught up on the debt Shane created, and my dad had several empty bedrooms. A few years earlier, he had built an over-sized five-bedroom, two-bathroom house, intending to flip it, but he still lives there to this day. When I moved in, he was living there alone.

6

The Aftermath of Leaving Shane

After my conversation with Shane, I left as quickly as I could—despite the fact it was only two days before his twenty-fifth birthday. It was the end of January, and I didn't want to start another year in misery. I left him with the reclining loveseat, big TV, entertainment cabinet, kitchen table set, air conditioner, and the desk that cost me $1000.

All I took was the bed—since it was originally mine—my dresser, and the small television. That was all the furniture we owned, and I let him keep most. I wanted to make sure he wouldn't struggle too hard without me.

I was still putting his needs ahead of my own.

I even paid his phone bill for the next four months, but that was unintentional. I called the phone company to tell them the phone would be switched into his name and to take my name off the account, which they did. When Shane called to activate it in his name, the operator asked whether the payment would be coming out of the same bank account, and he said yes. I didn't realize it until I switched banks and the withdrawal bounced.

I wasn't impressed with my phone company or Shane when I found out. Moving in with my father was awkward.

We didn't know how to talk to each other. I tried watching TV with him a couple of times, but we avoided each other for the most part. When I first moved in, I was still working at the magazine, so I was gone all day. After work, I would hang out at a friend's houses until it was late enough that I could feel certain my dad would already be in bed.

I didn't cut all ties with Shane in the beginning. We still talked and saw each other a few times a week. He wanted us to get back together. I was quickly losing weight and gaining confidence, which he seemed to appreciate. To be completely honest, since this book is my confessional, I was also still sleeping with him. He was the only man I knew intimately, and it was comforting.

In the beginning of March, after just over a month of living with my dad, I decided I had to leave my job at the magazine. I was the target of too many accusations since my friend's fallout, and two coworkers in particular were deliberately trying to sabotage my reputation. The stress of leaving Shane along with my bad job situation was destroying me.

I had quite a few clients at the magazine who wanted additional work, and my close friend from work—one of the few who believed my innocence—was an incredibly talented graphic design artist. I suggested that we start our own advertising agency. It was an ambitious venture for two women in their early twenties, but we were educated and experienced.

Finally being free from Shane initially gave me confidence and a sense of empowerment. I felt as if I was starting a new chapter in my life and that anything was possible. That attitude created the advertising business, but I didn't realize that I couldn't just snap my fingers for all my troubles to be gone. There was still a long road ahead of me before I would find success.

Despite being rent-free, I couldn't manage my massive debt without a more stable source of income. My mother worked at a machine shop with a cafeteria, so I was able to get a part-time position helping out during the busier times. I also went back to waitressing a few days a week. It was at a golf course, which turned out to very lucrative since I was losing weight and looking better than I had in the past.

In March, I also decided that I had to cut all ties with Shane. I went to visit him at our old apartment, and we were chatting about meaningless stuff when he quickly turned the conversation to sex. He wanted it, but this time he chose the wrong words to convey his interest.

"Damn, you look so good that I can't keep my hands off you. Why couldn't you have lost the weight while we were together?"

Ouch!

His question reminded me about all of the reasons that made it a bad relationship. The mental abuse, the fact that he didn't accept or appreciate who I was on the inside, and how he cared more about how I looked and what I could do for him then he did about me.

I responded calmly, "Why couldn't you love me the way I was?"

I immediately got off the couch, grabbed my purse, and made my way to the door. He begged and pleaded, claimed he always loved me, and that he never meant to hurt me, but I left. He even stood outside calling after me as I drove away, but I stayed strong.

I was finally learning that I deserved someone better than Shane.

My decision was later confirmed when I ended up hanging out with one of Shane's old college friends after bumping into him at a bar. He told me about Shane's coke habit and that Shane had cheated on me several times while we were together. He even specifically mentioned an incident when Shane had sex with some girl in a parking lot behind the bar, lost his Oakley sunglasses, and then bragged to his friends that I was dumb enough to help him search for them.

I was dumb, but fortunately I was no longer willing to let his behavior destroy me.

Shane kept calling me and stopping by uninvited, but I wouldn't answer the phone or the door. I even called his mom and told her that he needed to leave me alone or I would be forced to call the police. Like

Shane himself, his mom begged me to get back together with him. She was worried about him and felt that I could help him get back on track.

I was falling apart too, and I needed to break free from him completely.
I will never forget my last real interaction with Shane.

I've seen Shane three times since the incident on April 2, 2003. I saw him twice in Wal-Mart, when I ran in the opposite direction and then immediately left the store. The third time, I drove by him while he was waiting at a bus stop. I know we still live in the same city, but fortunately some higher power—thank you, God—has allowed me to escape him for the past ten years. I also have friends and family who will warn me if they see him working someplace, so I'll know what areas in the city I need to avoid.

I remember the date because it was the day after April Fools' Day, and at first I thought Shane was trying to play a joke on me. The phone rang at 7:10 am on a Tuesday morning. I was still in bed, but it kept ringing, so finally I got up to answer it. I didn't recognize the number on the display.

"Hey, we need to talk. I'm on my way."

It was Shane.

"No, don't come here."

"Hear me out, please. I'll be there in ten minutes."

"No Shane, I don't want to talk. We've said everything, and it is over."

"I'm already on my way."

Shane hung up. I wasn't dressed, so I quickly threw on some clothes, went to the washroom, and brushed my teeth. I looked out the living room window and didn't see him or his car, so I went outside. It took me less than three minutes, and I was at the door with my car keys in hand.

Unfortunately, I had to go upstairs in the living room to get a full look of the street, and by the time I went back down the stairs to get outside, he had shown up. When I turned around from locking the front door, he was already in the driveway and getting out of his car.

"Are you ready to go?"

"Yes, but I'm not going with you."

"After almost seven years, you can't get a coffee with me?"

"Shane, I have nothing to say to you."

"That's fair, but there are things I need to say to you. I get it now. Please, one coffee?"

I had no interest or intention of getting back together with him, but I was worried what he would do if I said no. He seemed calm, and I didn't want to set him off. I started thinking about all the past incidents, like the time when he threw my rear-view mirror out the window. He was standing next to the first decent car I had ever owned, and I was visualizing him smashing in the window.

So, I agreed to the coffee.

I also agreed to let him drive his car—as a way to protect my new vehicle—which was the second bad decision I made that morning. I am not sure why I wasn't more worried about protecting myself. We started heading toward the river, and I noticed we passed a Tim Horton's coffee shop.

"Why don't we stop there?"

"I like the one at the corner of Lauzon and Wyandotte better."

"Umm, okay?"

That one was only a couple of minutes down the road, so I wasn't really worried. We had only been driving for a few minutes, but so far that was the extent of our conversation. Shane just stared blankly at the road in front of him.

"So, what do you want to talk to me about?"

"Let's wait until we get our coffees."

"Okay, what else is new?"

"Not much."

He didn't ask what was new with me, which was fine. I didn't really want to share any details of my life with him. He didn't know about my two new part-time jobs or about the business. I didn't want to take the chance of him showing up where I worked and creating a scene.

We pulled into the coffee shop parking lot, and Shane went into the drive-thru lane.

"I thought we were going inside to talk?"

"No, I want to go to the beach."

"It's cold and miserable out. I would rather go inside."

To be honest, I wanted to go someplace public. No one would be at the beach. It was April and cloudy. I was starting to notice that Shane seemed out of sorts, and I was feeling more and more uncomfortable.

"Can we please go inside?"

"Our first date was at the beach, and I want to go back there."

It wasn't our first date that he was recalling, but it was the day he officially asked me to be his girlfriend. It was my seventeen birthday, about a month after we had met. It was incredibly romantic when it happened, and it created a tradition of late-night picnics at the beach together.

At that moment, I was wishing it never happened.

I didn't feel nostalgic or romantic, but I agreed. Something in my heart told me that this was not a good time to confront or reject him. We got our coffees, drove to the beach, and parked the car. I immediately got out of the car, figuring that it was safer than being trapped inside it with him.

Of course, Shane asked me to stay in the car, but I insisted that we talk outside.

This conversation happened over ten years ago, and I am pretty sure I am able to recall every word of it. It was one of those moments in my life that I can visualize completely. The sky was gray, the waves were wildly thrashing, and there was no one in sight.

"Just tell me what you need to say, because I have to go home and get ready for work."

"Okay, I know—here goes. Do you remember when you said that my band making it big would be like winning the lottery?"

"No. Why?"

"You know why. I finally figured it out. You didn't actually leave me. I know what you are doing."

"What?"

"I know that you have been working on promoting the band, and you've landed us a big contract. That's why you've been gone. You wanted it to be a surprise. You have been acting as my agent, and I'm not mad at you for it."

"What? That's not what's going on Shane. I have no idea what you are talking about."

"You don't have to hide it anymore. I know that you've turned my band into a huge success, and we have money now."

In the beginning of our conversation I was wandering a few feet away from him and trying not to make eye contact. At this point, I realized that he was covering his mouth during the entire conversation.

"Why are you covering your mouth?"

"Sssshhhhh, be careful—they can read your lips"

"Who?"

"They are watching us."

"Who is watching us?"

"You know who—they're everywhere. That's why I wanted to come here. I don't think they can hide very well in this big parking lot."

"Shane, what are you talking about?"

"You know what I am talking about."

"You are worrying me right now. I want to go home."

"You can't go home. You're coming home with me."

Finally, I screamed as loud as I could, "No! I am not. You are going to bring me to my dad's house right now and then get some help. We are done, and I can't deal with this anymore."

"What about the band?"

"Your band broke up a long time ago, and so did we. I am not trying to surprise you. We are over."

"Don't say that."

This time I screamed in his face, "It's true, and I want to go home now!"

Shane drop his hand from his mouth, shook his head repeatedly, and then stared off toward the beach. After a few minutes had passed, he seemed to snap out of the trance he was in. When he turned back toward me, I could see life in his eyes again. His eyes looked sad, but they looked more alive than they did a few minutes prior.

"Fine, I'll take you home."

He sounded defeated and deflated but believable.

"You need help, Shane—please."

"I know. Can we just go?"

I could tell Shane was embarrassed by what just happened. The look on his face reminded me of a small child who had just been caught with his finger inside his nose. I am not sure why I trusted him after the conversation we just had, but I got into the car, and we headed back to my dad's house. Before he dropped me off, I reminded him again that our relationship was over and that I didn't want him contacting me. He agreed—after accusing me of overreacting. He calmly pulled into my driveway, I insisted again that he stay out of my life, and I went inside.

That bizarre encounter was the last conversation I ever had with Shane.

7

Life without Shane

I was so shaken by Shane's behavior that I called his stepmom as soon as I got home. She suggested that he was still drunk from the night before and that was why he wasn't making any sense. I shared a few minor details from the last year of our life—not the smothering with the pillow—but enough other crazy incidents that it should have been clear that he was legitimately unstable and that I strongly felt he needed help. I asked her to please get him help before something horrible happened.

Once I cut ties with Shane, my life started to show some promise. I was looking more attractive than I had in the past (probably the hottest I'll ever look), and I was partying like a single woman for the first time in seven years. The ad agency my friend and I had started was landing some worthwhile clients, and I was making great tips at my part-time jobs.

I also was constantly being hit on at these jobs because they involved feeding and serving large groups of men. I had been in a serious and committed relationship since I was seventeen years old. I had forgotten how great it felt to be wanted. I welcomed the attention and quickly learned how to flirt back.

In all honesty, I wasn't really sought after by many guys before Shane, so the attention was completely new to me, and I loved it. I also loved wearing short skirts and tight shirts. Sexy clothes were new to me, since I recently had gone from weighing almost 190 pounds to a super-slim 135 pounds. This happiness was before I started to worry about the real reason behind how I was able to lose 55 pounds in six weeks without really dieting or exercising.

The first guy I dated after Shane was a good ole country boy named Jeffrey. He was the groundskeeper at the golf course where I was waitressing, and he seemed sweet and trustworthy. I didn't want any more drama from the men in my life. Unfortunately, I quickly learned that he was destined to be my rebound guy.

I wasn't attracted to him.

I was dating him because he asked nicely, and I didn't know how to say no. Most of the guys I met so far immediately tried for the one-night stand and were denied. I couldn't handle casual sex even during my wildest experiences as a single woman. Jeffrey was willing to go on a few dates before he made an attempt to take the relationship any further.

I also slept with him because he asked nicely, and I didn't know how to say no. I started spending time with him because he invited me to do things with him and I didn't have a reason to say no. I know now how ridiculous it sounds, but my confidence was still pretty tragic.

After a month or two of dating—I didn't keep track because I didn't really care—he invited me to an out-of-town wedding. Once again, I said yes. He was from a small town a few hours away, and we decided to spend the night at his parents' house.

I tried to get to know him on the three-hour drive to his parents' place, but deep down I wasn't really interested. I made my mind up that weekend that he wasn't the right guy for me and decided I needed to break up with him after we got back to Windsor.

It made me especially uncomfortable that his family gushed over me, since I already knew I had no intention of seeing them again. I also remember Jeffrey squeezing my hand during the wedding vows, which made me feel nauseated. He was falling for me, but I was not interested in the least.

The wedding reception was also a disaster. I remember it starting off okay, but I have no idea what happened after we sat down for dinner. I had two glasses of wine that I remember, and everything after that point is a blank. Jeffrey told me I danced and seemed normal, but I completely blacked out. I woke up naked in the bed next to Jeffrey, and my dress was hung neatly on the chair in front of me.

I didn't remember taking it off—or anything else that happened.

Part of me felt strongly that someone put something in my drink to knock me out and take advantage of me. Jeffrey's buddy had been very flirty with me prior to my blackout, and he had a creepy vibe about him. He was also the one who brought me the second glass of wine.

The other part of me thought of Shane. He always claimed he blacked out the night he smothered me with a pillow. Maybe he truly didn't realize he was doing it. The fact he almost killed me still haunts me, and it is the reason that I run in the opposite direction every time I see him. I'm not sure now how I lived with him for several months after it happened. It was pretty obvious that I didn't really didn't care for my own life at that time.

I care about my life right now, but I didn't during the time in my life that I am writing about in this confessional. My life lacked a purpose, since no one needed me anymore. My days were spent working hard, and my nights were spent stoned out of my mind. The awkward relationship with Jeffrey wasn't the only mistake I was making.

Marijuana had become my life.

I smoked it as soon as I could during the day, which meant booking any appointments with my ad agency clients first thing in the morning. I could waitress and work in the cafeteria stoned, but my business meant too much to me to jeopardize meeting with a client when I wasn't 100% sober. I needed marijuana just to function, and I even attempted to grow my own plant in the closet at my dad's house.

He actually caught me growing two marijuana plants. He let me know that he found them by leaving my closet and bedroom doors wide open. He had turned off the light system I hooked up. I immediately destroyed the plants in a panic and left the remnants in the pots where he could see it. We tried not to talk to each other, so this was our form of communication.

My fine role model of a father told me later on that he wasn't upset about the plants, and I didn't need to destroy them. He was just worried I might burn down the house and wanted me to rethink my lighting system.

Since this book is entitled *Dark Confessions*, I must admit that my marijuana habit also cost me over $3000 in one day. I know my family will be disappointed with me, but I promised myself that I would be completely honest. If I can admit to growing weed, I can also admit that it was the reason I destroyed the only brand-new car I have ever owned.

This is the same car I was so worried about Shane destroying in my dad's driveway.

I can drive stoned.

I don't recommend it, and I know in my heart that it's wrong, but I have been doing it most of my life, so it seems to come naturally. I can even—usually—roll a joint when I am driving, and I demonstrated this skill to my friends on more than one occasion. Sadly, I was quite proud of it.

When I was living with my dad, I avoided the house as much as possible. I had three jobs and a few reliable friends, so most days I had some place to go. Some days, I just drove around smoking in my car.

I ran up a median in a little subdivision while rolling a joint.

I had to clean up all the little pieces of marijuana before I could call a tow truck. Unfortunately, my luck was pretty bad at that point in my life. I am not sure if it was karma, fate, or God trying to teach me a lesson, but my front tire went flat, so my airbags went off, which caused the front window to shatter in a thousand pieces. The mechanic also said that there was a knick on the engine, and since the car was brand new, it would need to be replaced.

My $21,000 Ford Focus that I just bought four months earlier was a write-off. Since cars depreciate the moment you drive them off the lot, I only received $16,800 for it. The check I received for the car didn't cover the balance I still owed on it. Unfortunately, it wasn't the wake-up call I desperately needed. As usual, it takes me a few tries before I clue into life's most important lessons.

I made new friends who were just as much in love with my favorite drug. One was a waitress where I worked, and the other was her best friend. They were very different from my usual friends, who had mostly abandoned me within the last year or two of my life.

As I mentioned earlier, I got into a horrible fight with my oldest and life-long best friend Samantha a couple years prior because she had seen Shane's bad side when we lived together and she wanted me to leave him. She was always around us, so she witnessed him calling me names, punching walls, and throwing dishes. The fight was awful, but fortunately everything was put behind us about a year after I left Shane.

I didn't have Samantha, and I didn't have the friend that lied to me about forging the advertising contracts. My new work schedule conflicted with those of two of my other friends—I worked nights; they worked days—and they felt that I was changing. They would get together without me, and somehow they determined that my new weight loss had made me conceded and self-centered.

I probably did change because I was sick. I just didn't know it yet. I was also living in a fast-paced, drug-induced coma, so I could have been unbearable. I honestly only remember the highlights—and lowlights—from that year of my life. My daily encounters and personal behavior are a blur.

It had been the most traumatic year of my life, and my life before Shane already felt like a cruel joke. Everything I just went through with Shane and my job, and now my friends had given up on me. I had one close friend left—my business partner—and she had her own life to deal with and her own drama. I had no one to lean on, so I had to make new friends.

I couldn't handle being alone.

After only knowing these new friends for about a month or two, the opportunity came up to go to Vegas with them. It would be two couples and me, so I was the fifth wheel, but it would still be worth it. I deserved a vacation from reality, and these were the perfect people for one. It was mid-May when we booked everything, and the trip was scheduled for July 28. I started spending all my free time with my new friends, whose forms of entertainment were significantly different than what I usually did with my friends.

Tina and Krissie really liked to party.

They knew how to have fun, which sometimes involved dressing in tight little dresses and hanging out at female strip clubs. The guys at the club would buy our drinks, so it truly was a great idea. Windsor has some of the world's finest all-nude clubs, and I've visited many of them throughout my life.

Prior to leaving Shane, the only time I ever set foot in one was when I was selling advertising space for the magazine. Now, I was going there for a fun night out. I even once wore a tiny white dress while splashing around in a kiddie pool on stage at a strip club with two naked women and my new best friends. That was definitely one of the wildest things I have ever done, and I honestly have no reason to regret it. I was being adventurous and going with the flow.

It was during this period of my life that I truly learned to live without regret.

I had the right outlook on life, but I didn't know how to have it without destroying myself in the process. I recently lost fifty-five pounds without effort, but that wasn't the only sign that something was wrong with my health. I wasn't able to sleep unless I was completely stoned, my eyes looked like they were bursting from their sockets, and my hair was falling out.

The worst part was how my heart would race uncontrollably without warning—and then suddenly stop. I would be lying in bed, listening to my heart beat so hard and fast that I thought it would burst from my chest, and then it would suddenly skip several beats. I knew something wasn't right, but I just ignored it.

I ignored the symptoms for a few months, but they kept getting worse. I finally started to worry when I noticed a bald patch on my scalp. I wasn't worried about being sick until it started to affect my appearance negatively. My new-found body was making me quite vain. I had no problem accepting the unexplained weight loss or heart trouble, but noticeable hair loss made me seek help immediately.

I mentioned what was going on to my mom, who immediately knew the underlying cause. She went through it herself fifteen years earlier when she left my dad. My mom had ongoing hyperthyroidism issues, and I was showing significant signs of it.

Unfortunately, I didn't have a doctor at the time. My previous doctor had a few malpractice claims against him and left the city suddenly. I didn't bother to replace him, since I wasn't really concerned about my own wellbeing.

I put off seeing a doctor for a few more weeks until my mom started insisting on it. She helped me get an appointment with her doctor. Her doctor ran a bunch of tests and called me two days later for a follow-up. It was hyperthyroidism, and it was severe. It was so bad that it had developed into Graves disease, and I was at high risk of congestive heart failure.

It was a Friday, and my new doctor booked me an appointment with a thyroid specialist for that following Monday. She was able to get me an appointment so quickly, because my results were so alarming. Unfortunately, I was leaving for Las Vegas on Monday. When I told her I couldn't make the appointment, she lectured me on my priorities and tried to scare me into cancelling my trip. She was especially concerned because I was going to Vegas.

"No alcohol, no caffeine, no stimulants of any sort. You must take it easy. Your heart is very fragile."

Even as she was giving it, I knew I wasn't going to follow her advice, but I nodded along. I was going to Vegas with four people who loved to party. There was no chance that I wasn't going to drink alcohol, and I was certain they had no intentions of taking it easy.

I had no intention of surviving Vegas, and I almost didn't.

I was so sick of where my life was headed that I wrote another goodbye letter before we left, in the morbid hope that the Graves disease would finally put me out of my misery. This letter was just for my family and friends. Shane's name was not mentioned.

Something in my heart is telling me I won't be coming back from Vegas. The last few years of my life have exhausted me and I'm not sure I

can handle much more. I'm ready. Please know that I went out smiling.
Love always.

I placed it in an envelope on the driver's seat of my car, which would be parked in front of Tina's house while we were in Vegas. I was fine with the idea of dying like a rock star while partying in Vegas. I kept both goodbye letters for several years as a reminder of how little I used to value my life compared with how much I treasure it now.

Once again, this book is a confessional, and I must admit another poor decision I made in my past. We needed marijuana for the trip and couldn't guarantee that we would get enough to handle our habit while we were in Vegas. Tina and Krissie were both moms, and the guys they brought with them were dads. I was single with no kids, which meant I had the least to lose. I was also the fifth wheel for the trip, so I volunteered.

I agreed to smuggle about $200-worth of marijuana in my carry-on bag. We were 'smart' about it—well as smart as you can be when you take the chance of smuggling drugs across the Canada–US border and then smuggling them onto a plane that is flying from Detroit to Las Vegas.

We condensed the pot into a long tube shape and hid it inside a pink balloon, which was placed inside a solid pink bottle of Herbal Essence conditioner. All you saw was pink conditioner when you took the cap off the bottle. I had an innocent-looking appearance and felt the plan was pretty safe. Fortunately, I was right.

The first day in Las Vegas was exhilarating.

It was better than I ever dreamed a vacation could be, since prior to this I could only afford weekend getaways in Ontario. We toured all of the impressive hotels, drank plenty of yummy drinks, ate incredible food, and hung out together by the pool. It was my first real vacation, and I was enjoying every second of it. The second day started off just as great, but it took an unexpected wrong turn just after we ate dinner.

All five of us took a cab to the Rio. We were staying at the MGM Grand, which was on the Strip, and the Rio was not. It was too far away for us to walk there, especially since it was now night time. We watched the impressive Mardi Gras parade in the lobby and then went to the bar on the roof of the hotel. As far as I could tell, everyone was getting along and having a great time. I was on the lookout for hot guys, so I wasn't paying much attention to the happy couples.

Tina approached me when we were upstairs and said that we were going back to the Strip. I could see Krissie at the other end of the bar with her husband, but I followed Tina and Ryan to the elevator. I asked Tina on the elevator why they weren't coming with us, and she said they would meet up with us later. There was an incredibly attractive fitness buff on the elevator, so I forgot about Krissie and started flirting with him.

Surprisingly, he was interested in me. He even paid for our cab back to the hotel.

He also invited me to play some high-stakes Black Jack with him. Tina and Ryan said they were going up to the room to relax, and since the night was still young, I followed the hunk into the high-rollers section of the MGM Grand.

I was having fun gambling his money away until Krissie saw me.
She stormed over to our table and started screaming.

"How dare you leave us at the Rio; we had to pay for a cab all by ourselves. Who do you think you are?"

"What? Tina said you knew we were leaving."

"Well, she was wrong."

Krissie was a tough woman, and I was seriously afraid of what she could do to me, especially when she was that upset and drunk. Ugly memories of Shane's temper were causing me to tremble. Fortunately she believed me somewhat and settled down slightly. I didn't know until later that Tina and Krissie had a fight at the Rio, which was why Tina wanted to leave so suddenly.

"Well, you and Tina can spend the rest of the weekend without me. You picked your side."

Krissie and her husband took off, and I didn't see them again until the flight home. The scene she created in front of my sexy new friend was embarrassing, so I excused myself to the bathroom as soon as Krissie was out of sight.

In the washroom I realized the fitness hunk was probably expecting sex from me, since I was so willing to accept his generosity. It hadn't occurred to me earlier, since I still viewed myself as being fat and undesirable. I couldn't imagine a fitness instructor wanting to be with me. Once I looked in the bathroom mirror, I was reminded that I was only 135 pounds, which was skinny for my body type.

This man could actually want to have sex with me.

I had only been intimate with Shane and Jeffrey. I didn't feel safe sleeping with some random man I met in Vegas, so I went up to the hotel room that I was sharing with Tina and Ryan. I didn't bother to say goodbye to my hot new friend.

They were both asleep when I got there. I spent most of the day drinking, so I felt drunk and depressed lying in the bed next to the happy couple. I was spending money I couldn't afford, I didn't trust men anymore, and I wasn't thrilled with my new choice of friends. My heart started to race rapidly out of control. It was beating so hard that I felt pain radiating throughout my body.

All of a sudden my heart stopped.

I was searching my wrist and neck for a pulse, but I couldn't feel it beating. This had happened before, but it usually started beating again after a few seconds. Seconds felt like minutes. I should have called out to Tina and Ryan, but I didn't. I didn't fight to live this time. I simply closed my eyes and prayed this was the end. This is how I predicted it would be before I got on the plane. I close my eyes and then the nightmare is finally over.

I was ready.

Surprisingly, I didn't die in my sleep like I was expecting. Instead, I woke up feeling relieved and reenergized. I knew the moment I woke up that I was not meant to die tragically young. There were so many situations where I should have died throughout the last year of my life, yet I survived all of them.

I had a purpose.

I would like to think that purpose is to write a novel that inspires women who are in abusive relationships to leave their abuser. I also hope that I am able to remind people that we are in control of our own lives. We can't allow the tragedies that will inevitably enter our lives be the death of us.

That is what happened to Shane.

He had promise and a charming personality. He was smart and a talented musician. He could have had a very bright future. Instead he allowed his life to get worse and worse. He refused help when it was offered, and he felt the tragedies he went through justified his downfall.

I spent the next two days wandering around Vegas by myself. I suntanned by the pool, danced on top of the bar at Coyote Ugly, and met some entertaining new friends. I was ready to start enjoying my life, but unfortunately I didn't have very much money left. I will admit to stealing in Vegas, but that was honestly the last time I stole anything.

Surviving Vegas gave me a conscience.
I made a commitment to myself that I was going to live a better life.

I was going to start paying down my debt, put more energy into making the business a success, and try to get through the day sober instead of living in a cloud of intoxicating smoke. I made the transition from that lost little girl in Vegas to the strong confident woman who finished a marathon by taking it one step at a time.

The first step is always the hardest.
There was no overnight miracle.

It was almost six years later before I finally quit smoking and started to make healthier choices. I was 150 pounds when I got married in 2006, and I was happy with the way I looked. Sadly I slowly started to gain back the weight. A few months before my thirtieth birthday (in 2009), I got on the scale and saw an alarming 185 pounds. Although I was in a healthy relationship with my loving and supportive husband, my self-esteem issues started to reappear. I was jealous of any woman who talked to my husband, despite the fact that I trusted him. I was also allowing my boss at the time to verbally abuse and manipulate me.

I was repeating former patterns of self-destruction.
That was when I made the commitment to run a marathon.
Setting goals and achieving them turned my life around.

The only goal I had when I first got home from Vegas in 2003 was to become healthy, but I wasn't strong enough to tackle all of my bad habits. I first sought treatment for my thyroid issue and then used a few different daily self-affirmations to rebuild my self-esteem. I was once a confident woman with great determination. I needed to revive that part of myself.

I also decided that I needed to officially end it with Jeffrey. Technically, we were still together, and I could tell he was falling in love with me. I avoided him the few weeks before Vegas, but I hadn't ended it. The truth needed to be said.

Sadly, I still didn't have the guts to say it out loud.
I wrote him a break-up letter and put it in his mailbox.

The letter was brutally honest. I'm a writer, and it was easy to express—on paper—how I was feeling. I had enough self-awareness to know that I didn't have the strength to stand my ground in a verbal confrontation. I'm a people-pleaser. I knew that I would cave if Jeffrey tried to convince me to stay. I was finally accepting my weaknesses and learning how to work around them.

Jeffrey died in a motorcycle accident the following year.
His new girlfriend was on the back of the bike, but she survived.

I did not stay in touch with Jeffrey or even talk to him after I dropped off the letter. I started waitressing at a different golf course and avoided anything connected with him or that time in my life, including my new friends Tina and Krissie. My mother saw the article about Jeffrey's accident in the *Windsor Star* newspaper. I hope and pray his new girlfriend had the strength to deal with losing him. He was a nice guy.

I know I would not have had the strength at that time in my life if I was still with him.

Everything happens for a reason.

A few months after my eye-opening morning in Vegas, I received a frantic call from Shane's mother, who said that he had been hospitalized. He had driven his truck to Ingersoll—three hours from Windsor—in the middle of the night and then called her saying he lost his truck, his clothes, his shoes, and his wallet. He also didn't know how he got there, and he was scared.

Shane's mom begged me to go with her to the hospital. She wanted me to see him, so I could help bring the old Shane back. She insisted that all Shane needed was to have me back in his life. After much debate and her desperate guilt trips, I gave in slightly. I decided I would go with her to the hospital, but I would not go inside.

I did not want to see Shane. I was afraid of him, especially after she told me that, prior to leaving for Ingersoll, he had had a violent fit during which he had destroyed his guitar and amps with a baseball bat.

I had already survived enough of Shane's violent fits.

I waited for over an hour in the parking lot of the hospital. It was the same hospital that I spent a week at when Shane's father was dying. I paced back and forth next to her car as I chain-smoked obsessively. I was relieved that he was getting help yet I panicked that I would be forced back into his life.

I still hadn't realized that no one could force me to stay with someone.

I think Shane's mother purposely stayed up there with him for such a long time because she was hoping I would get frustrated and go inside to find out what was taking her so long. She wasn't a very compassionate mother prior to this incident, and I doubt she was being that way now.

I couldn't see Shane. I was just starting to get my hyperthyroidism under control, and I couldn't get sucked back into his drama. I knew trying to save Shane again would be the death of me, and it was the first time I had liked my life in the last four years. Although I sincerely cared about how Shane was doing, I finally realized that I cared about my own health even more.

That was when I knew I was a new me.

8

A New Life with a New Me

Over the course of my life, I have made many excuses for my past mistakes and bad behavior, for Shane's mistakes and bad behavior, and for my parent's mistakes and bad behavior. We had bad parents, we were young, it was the environment we lived in—these are the lies we tell ourselves so we don't feel bad about our prior poor judgment. It wasn't until I realized that I was in control of my life that I started to make good decisions.

I stole because I wanted to be cool. I also wanted nice stuff and money for alcohol and drugs. I smoked pot to be cool and to escape the troubles that were plaguing my life. I lied to get away with the things I was doing, and I willingly stayed with Shane despite knowing how dangerous he could be.

I was responsible for where my life had ended up.
No one else is to blame for the failures in my life, and no one else can be credited with the good I have now accomplished.
This is my life.

I once was too ashamed of my life to take responsibility for it, but now I am proud to say I am in control of my life. That doesn't mean I have it all figured out and no longer make poor decisions. I've just realized that I am the one responsible for my actions. Right or wrong, I am in charge of the path I am on and how I respond to road bumps along the way.

I am the reason I am successful.

When I first announced I was going to walk a half-marathon, many people in my life rightfully doubted me. I smoked half a pack a day, and I was 50 pounds overweight. Their doubt motivated me. I quit smoking three months later, lost 20 pounds, and finished a half-marathon six months after I set the goal.

I felt so empowered by my accomplishment that I vowed to run a full marathon the following year. I lost another 20 pounds, worked out like a madwoman, and finished my first full marathon in 2010. I didn't run the entire way—in fact, I struggled through most of it—and I wanted to quit at several points along the way. One foot in front of the other, I kept moving forward until I crossed the finished line. I accomplished my goal one step at a time.

I am the reason I am happy.

The many wonderful people I have met in my life contribute to that happiness, but I choose to be around them. I now have a loving and supportive husband, I have a great relationship with almost all of my family (my father being the only exception), and all my old friends are back in my life, except for a few that I chose not to be around. I also have a healthy body and—more importantly—a healthy body image.

This didn't instantly happen.

It was a long and slow journey that included many challenging obstacles. The ups and downs of my professional career and adjusting to the role of stepmom have granted me almost as much drama and heartbreak as Shane did.

I could (and may) write a sequel on the missteps of the last ten years, like calling my boss an "ego-testical prick" and being escorted off of the premises. I redeveloped my backbone, but unfortunately it took me a while before I learned how to use it appropriately. My boss had earned that nasty comment, but I handled the situation poorly.

I've made bad choices since my wake-up call in Vegas, but I truly value my life now. I will continue to make mistakes because I am human, but at least now I try to learn from them instead of beating myself up for making them. I am not perfect.

My life is not perfect.

I don't expect my life to be perfect. I embrace the flaws in myself, in others, and in life. Bad things still happen, and I can't control when others create negativity in my life. I can only control how I react. I choose to find the reason behind the madness of the world we live in. I now understand that I don't need to expect the worse and just give up on life every time that something devastating happens. Living in fear of the future is a horrible way to live.

Everything happens for a reason.
Things get better with time.

I was nervous about writing this book because of how it will affect Shane. I've changed his name and minor details, but he will obviously know that it is about him. I also recently discovered that he is still unstable and under psychiatric care. I don't want to hurt him or hinder his progress, but it is not my responsibility to protect him from the life he has led.

Shane saved my life by telling me the truth and pointing out that I needed to leave him for my own well-being. Maybe this book can be his wake-up call. His life once had great potential and hopefully by reading this, it will inspire him to find himself again. Either way, the six and a half years that I spent with Shane taught me that I need to take care of myself first and that I wasn't responsible for his life.

I was responsible for my life.

I also felt responsible for sharing my stories with others who are suffering through similar situations. So many people hide abuse out of shame or fear. Not telling people about Shane's behavior made it easier for me to rationalize and justify it. My silence almost cost me my life, and I refuse to stay silent anymore.

I can help other women see a bright future despite the clouds.

This book is called *Dark Confessions of an Extraordinary, Ordinary Woman* because, although my tale of survival is extraordinary, the problems I faced in my life are unfortunately way too ordinary. My mother, my mother-in-law, and many of my friends have similar experiences.

So many women put up with abuse because they don't have the confidence to stand up for themselves. They willingly put someone else's needs and happiness ahead of their own. They feel trapped. They feel responsible for the other person's survival. They give countless reasons why they can't leave and make a million excuses for how they are being treated.

The tragedies in Shane's life were no excuse for his behavior.
Everyone endures tragedy in life.

Shane was not the only person to suffer loss. I have two friends who lost both of their parents when they were tragically young. Both of these women have incredibly productive and happy lives. I have a friend who lost her best friend in a tragic car accident when she was a teenager and then the same friend lost her sister in just as horrible of an accident a few years later. She has an incredibly productive and happy life. I know women who were brutally bullied, women who were raped, and women who were in abusive relationships far worse than mine. They all survived and have happy lives. Their tragedies are not an excuse to stop living a good life.

The life you are living now doesn't need to be the life you will always live.

So many women feel trapped. I mentioned a friend much earlier in the novel that was also my business partner. I said she was the only one who was there for me, but she had drama in her own life. Her husband was similar to Shane, except without any of the physical abuse. He had drug addiction issues—he was lazy and irresponsible, and he couldn't keep a job.

She is talented, hard-working, and beautiful—inside and out. She deserved better than him, but she felt trapped because they had twin boys together. Her relationship was a slightly twisted version of Shane and me.

Instead of her husband being the one to suffer loss, she was the one hurting over the loss of loved ones. She is the same person I mentioned a few paragraphs ago that lost a close friend and then her sister in tragic car accidents. She once told me that she didn't feel strong enough to leave her husband.

Her life was just as heartbreaking as Shane's, but she didn't use it as an excuse to not be productive and kind.

She was also like me, because she put her husband's needs ahead of her own. She worried because she knew he couldn't take care of himself. She was married to him for nine years before she realized that her own happiness mattered. She finally left him just over a year ago, and I have never seen her happier. She could write her own novel.

My story is not rare.

Over the last few years, I have met many women with similar stories of being empowered by adversity. One of the girls that walked me home in grade school when my first boyfriend beat my face in with a metal bar has a story that almost mimics my own. She survived a tragic love story that inspired her to change her life. She is now in the best mental, emotional, and physical shape of her life. She even recently finished a marathon.

Everyone has the power to achieve greatness.

Writing this confessional took over a year, and I experienced self-doubt at several points along the way. I have more self-confidence now than I ever did, but having enough confidence to believe you can write a novel worthy of publishing requires a real ego. I believed in myself enough to invest my valuable time. I just need reassurance.

That was why I sought feedback.

As I sent this novel to other women in my life for their perspective, I discovered we all went down similar paths. Everyone survived their own form of abuse, anguish, anxiety, depression, or tragedy. My favorite response came from one of my aunts, who simply said my book was "a very typical coming of age story not much like mine but yet very much like mine!"

Statistics say that one in four women experience some form of abuse by someone they trust.
I believe it. I just don't understand why we allow it.
Women are stronger than they realize.

I was stronger than I realized. I almost gave up on my life because I thought my life was unbearable and unfair. I felt sorry for myself and thought no one in the world has it as bad as me. There were too many times in my life that I thought it would be easier to die than it would be to continue struggling. Yet I had the power to change my situation. I was strong enough to get out at any time, I just didn't know it. I now drive along the riverfront blasting motivational songs by strong women, like Katy Perry's *Roar* or Sara Bareilles' *Brave*.

I am inspired by other strong women.

I've since realized that my mother was and is a strong woman. Her life didn't go as planned, but she kept pushing forward. She always did the best she could, regardless of the situation. As soon as I asked her for support, she was there for me emotionally, mentally, and financially. She accepted my flaws and forgave my past mistakes, which was everything I needed from my mom.

I know she worries that I hold her responsible for some of what I endured, but I don't. She was actually the person responsible for my career as a writer. When I was in grade school, I read a short story and a few poems that she wrote. That was when I first fell in love with writing. I can blame heredity for my hyperactive thyroid, big thighs, and overactive tear ducts, but I also inherited my mother's talent for writing.

My parents are not responsible for the choices I made.
Thankfully I learned to make better choices.

I am confident that my husband will never put me through the same pain that Shane did. He watched his mother suffer at the hands of his abusive father, and he could never do that to any woman. He hasn't spoken to his dad for over twenty years. And even if my husband did abuse me, I know I could walk away the very first time and never look back.

I will not make that mistake again.

I also learned how to handle obstacles. I no longer fear challenges or chaos. I know I will survive, so I push through them with a smile and an optimistic outlook. I know nothing could happen to me now that would even make me consider giving up on my life. If I would have let Shane take my life or if I had taken my own life, I would have missed out on some of the most incredible experiences imaginable.

Suicide is a permanent solution to a temporary problem.

I would not have met my wonderful husband, watched four amazing children grow up, or finally achieved my dream of becoming a professional writer. I would have missed out on exciting vacations, camping trips, bonfires, birthday celebrations, and holiday dinners. I would have missed out on real happiness.

I also never would have found myself.

I am an outspoken and passionate person who uses social media to promote happiness and peace. I am an advocate of healthy living who has finished two marathons and a dozen smaller charity runs. I have two adorable black Labradors that make me laugh daily, and I am truly happy with all aspects of my life.

There was a time when a happy future seemed impossible, and now it is my reality. Anything is possible once you learn to believe in yourself.

It won't happen instantly. Hard work, determination, and commitment are necessary to accomplish the truly worthwhile goals in life. Once I learned to believe in myself, I was willing to put in the effort to improve my life and chase my dreams. Once I decided to finish a marathon, I forced myself to train five days a week. Once I made the commitment to write a novel, I poured my heart and soul into it. Once I took my first step toward happiness, I never looked back.

Although I think I am pretty special, there is nothing special about me. I was a deceptive and depressed young adult who didn't feel worthy of having a good life. My life is now better than good—it's incredible. If my life can be turned around, then there is hope for everyone. Everyone has the ability to change his or her life.

I started this novel quoting classic clichés, and I can't help but finish it the same way.

Dreams do come true.
Never give up.

Life is a Marathon

By Jenn Sadai

Life is a continuous path laid in front of us.

It stretches on for miles and miles, with no end in sight.

You'll never be certain where it is headed or how long it will take to get there.

Just keep moving forward one step at a time.

The path is filled with sudden twists and turns that can quickly knock you off course.

Tree branches, boulders, hills, and valleys will try to stand in your way.

The sun will go down, and the path will be overshadowed in darkness.

Just keep moving forward one step at a time.

Dramatic inclines and uneven ground will strain your tired muscles.

Your shoulders will ache from carrying the regrets of wrong turns made along the way.

Your feet will throb from walking, and you'll long for a chance to rest.

Just keep moving forward one step at a time.

People will try to drag you away from the path; others will push you forward.

You'll meet traveling companions that will lessen your load and some that will weigh you down.

You'll see wonders that you never imagined and sights you wish to quickly forget.

Just keep moving forward one step at a time.

Life is a marathon.

You were meant to live every moment of it until you reach the finish line.

Embrace the challenge, face the darkness, and climb the mountains fearlessly.

Soak in the scenery, enjoy the experience, and keep moving forward one step at a time.

About the Author

Writing has always been a creative outlet for Jenn Sadai. When her first short story was printed (she was fourteen), Jenn knew she wanted to become a writer and publish her very own novel.

Jenn Sadai was born and raised in Windsor, Ontario, where she attended St. Clair College of Applied Arts and Technology. This experience transformed her writing talent into a marketable skill, and she became a successful copywriter. It wasn't until her uncle's battle with leukemia that Jenn realized she was no longer following her dream of becoming a published author. After spending countless hours at the hospital talking with her uncle, Jenn quit her day job to pursue the career she always wanted.

Becoming a freelance writer was a scary move for Jenn, but support from family and friends spurred her on, and she continues to love every moment of it. Jenn is happily married with four wonderful stepchildren, and her dream of becoming a published author is finally a reality.

Watch for

DIRTY SECRETS OF THE WORLD'S WORST EMPLOYEE— THE OTHER SIDE OF THE STORY!

During her brief stint in the corporate world, the author worked for thirteen different employers. Very few of these jobs ended peacefully. Thankfully, unlucky number thirteen was the last straw that inspired her to become her own boss and pursue writing as a career.

CPSIA information can be obtained
at www.ICGtesting.com
Printed in the USA
LVOW07s1749200817
545702LV00001B/60/P